Splendour of Swaras

M. BALAMURALIKRSHNA

Splendour of Swaras

An Authorised Biography

By

'Kala Bharati'
B.M. Sundaram

SIDDHI

SIDDHI BOOKS

Imprint of

COSMO PUBLICATIONS

1996 INDIA

First Cosmo Edition 1996

ISBN 81-7020-716-9

Cover Photo: Sangeet Natak Academy
Inside Photo: Author

Published by:
MRS. RANI KAPOOR
***For* SIDDHI BOOKS**
Imprint of
COSMO PUBLICATIONS
***For* GENESIS PUBLISHING PVT. LTD.**
24-B, Ansari Road,
Darya Ganj,
New Delhi-110002. INDIA

Typeset by:
Manav Computer House
Delhi

Printed at:
Mehra Offset Press
Delhi

Foreword

Dr. M. Balamuralikrshna
No.3. Kanakasri Nagar,
Cathedral Road, Madras-600 086

Date 10-11-95

My Dear Sundaram,

I have gone through my biography written by you. You have covered all the important points and I appreciate your work and your sincere interest with which you have undertaken and completed this authentic biography of mine.

I approve it for publication.

With blessings,

Yours ever,

'Kala Bharati',
B. M. Sundaram,
Musicologist,
54, Ramakrishna Nagar,
Pondicherry-605003

Foreword

Dr. M. Balamuralikrishna
No. 3. Kanakasri Nagar,
Cathedral Road, Madras 600 086

Date: 10-11-98

My Dear Sundaram,

I have gone through my biography written by you. You have covered all the important points and I appreciate your work and your sincere interest with which you have undertaken and completed this authentic biography of mine.

I approve it for publication.

With Blessings,

Yours ever,

[illegible]
B. M. Sundaram,
Musicologist,
54 Ramakrishna Nagar,
Pondicherry 605003

Prologue

This is a biography of a most versatile musician-composer of this century. His accomplishments are myriads in number, although it may not be humanly possible to enumerate all of them. An earnest attempt to do, as best as my limited capability could, has bloomed as this work. Most of the material found in these pages are mainly from two sources: (a) Information provided by Mangalampalli Paṭṭabhiramayya, as and when sought and (b) My personal knowledge, through my intimate and long association with the celebrity. I also acknowledge with gratitude, some data have been collected from *Saptaswaralu* a book by M. Suryanarayana.

Dr. M. Balamuralikrshna is my venerable guru, but this work picturises him, least from the angle of a disciple and more from the view of a musicologist.

I profusely thank Cosmo Publications, Delhi, for having entrusted to me the privileged job of preparing this biography and their bringing this out in an excellent manner. I hope, I have done justice, since the 'SPLENDOUR OF SWARAS' is going to help the present generation and the posterity, as a glorious history, containing nothing but facts about this most illustrious son of India.

— B.M. SUNDARAM

Contents

Soaring Up High at the Sanctum of Music

It is shivering cold all around. The mercury has nearly reached thc freezing point, because it is the very first month of the year. Darkness has not departed completely and dawn was only now beginning to pierce the night, sending its faint, filtered light. The Sun, as if himself dreaded to venture into this cold, tries to appear insignificantly. Even in this darkness, the place is very active with surging crowds, at this early hour. Without minding the frosty cold, on this fifth day of the year, 1942, ladies and gents, neatly dressed or wearing a variety of ornaments are marching towards a temple, situated here. Many musicians, after finishing their morning ablutions very early today, are hurrying. They are not to be seen in their shirts, but they have covered their bodies with golden-lace bordered upper garments. Their foreheads glitter with their religious marks. Some among them are holding musical instruments. This place called Tiruvaiyaru or Panchanada Kshetra, is situated on the banks of the holy river, Kaveri, at a distance of about twelve kilometers from Tanjavur, the erstwhile city of Culture. The temple, where all these enter is the *Samadhi* of Sri Tyagaraja, the great composer.

Sri Tyagaraja (1767-1847), one among the Carnatic Musical Trinity, was a *nadopasaka*. He lived as an example to what he preached and attained eternal rest, on the Pushya Bahula Panchami day. His mortal remains were interred in this place and a small temple has been erected. People from all over the country assemble here, every year, to witness the rituals in connection with his *aradhana* performed on this day and to taste the sumptuous feast of music, distributed as an homage by the fraternity of Tyagaraja's grand disciples and others of that tribe. This year, the *aradhana* has been scheduled to take place on this fifth day January (1942).

The *shamiana*, in front of the Saint's *samadhi* is already crowded. The people who managed to get a seat, are looking around, with an anxiety, whether they could move forward and place themselves in the vicinity of the performing musicians. In the center of the *shamiana*, a special enclosure has been earmarked for the partaking musicians, who are arriving and occupying their seats. The choral singing is to be commenced shortly. Palladam Sanjeevi Rao, the seniormost flutist and one of his disciples, start to play the *kriti*, 'Chetulara' of Tyagaraja. Then the vocalists commence to sing in chorus, the *Pancharatna Kritis* (five compositions of Tagaraja, among his many, attributed as 'gems') and it is really a exhilirating experience to hear this choral-singing. Almost all the front ranking musicians of the Carnatic music world are here. At the end of the choral rendering, each one begins to sing, individually. They seem to be vigilant not to miss this rare opportunity; it would be their fortune, even if they sing one piece in such a sacred ambience. A competitive spirit of one to excel the other is also not lacking. One musician goes on rendering *kriti* after *kriti*, without any intermission, so that some one else may usurp his chance. There, there is sitting one elderly man, with a moustache on his face with an young boy on his lap. He is every now and then, signalling to the boy to start singing. Is it not surprising to see this old man, nodding to the boy, who may not have reached his tenth year and who could not be expected to know what singing is? But the boy's face exhibits confidence and enthusiasm. Whenever he tries to open his mouth, some one else commences in a stentorian voice. With a sort of frustration, the boy takes out fillip, with his fingers, Oh! Now there is a pause and availing it, he begins with the *kriti*, 'Manasa Sri Ramachandruni' in *Eesamanohari raga*. What a wonder! Every human form sitting in the lengthy *shamiana*, have turned as mere statues. Quietitude is everywhere. Nobody came forward to start singing, after this boy. Yes! They are drowned in his soul-stirring music. The crowd, with a desire to see the boy closer, start to move forward, while many stand up. The *vidwans*, occupying the front row, turn their heads, backward, to see the face of the boy. The moustached gentleman, understanding the people's enthusiasm, lifts up the boy, all along sitting on his lap, above his head, so that all could have a good look at him. Surprise is brimful on the faces of the people. They feel it is only supernatural for a young boy of about ten years, to sing so sweetly. The proceedings of the festival has now come to stop, due to this pandemonium. The organisers have a word with the moustached man and announce loudly: "This boy, who sang so wonderfully and melodiously is the son of Mangalampalli Pattabhiramayya of Bezawada. His name is Balamurali-krshna. This *vidwan*, having a moustache, is well known to many of us — Parupalli Ramakrshnayya Pantulu and the boy is his disciple. We very well know your interest in hearing this boy and would definitely try to accommodate his programme on one of these days. We request you to be calm and quiet and to co-operate in our going ahead with other functions".

Kings and Nobles, according to history, patronised music and musicians to a great extent. But, the fame of such persons is only inferior to that of 'Vidyasundari' Bangalore Nagartnamma, who raised a temple for Sri Tyagaraja, at Tiruvaiyaru, dedicating all her property to the maintenance and functioning of the temple.

Born in Nanjangudu, near Mysore, on 3.11.1878, she became adept in Vocal music, Dancing, Sanskrit and Telugu. She lived in Madras and after the construction of the temple at Tiruvaiyaru, she moved over to that place and spent days there till her end on 19.5.1952.

It is fitting that her mortal remains were also interred, opposite to the shrine of Tyagaraja. Before her, the *aradhana*, in the form the *Samadhi Pooja* was begun by Tillaisthanam Rama Iyengar and Umayalpuram Sundara Bhagavater brothers, all the direct disciples of Tyagaraja. The *Aradhana* festival, in a grand manner was commenced by Tillaisthanam Narasimha Bhagavater and his younger brother, Panju Bhagavatar, in 1906. Thence, Tiruvaiyaru became a sacred center for the lovers of Carnatic music.

The Silver Jubilee celebrations of Andhra Maha Sabha, Madras, was celebrated on 28.12.1941. Young Balamuralikrshna's vocal recital was also slated in the cultural programmes and at the same time, the boy had a broadcasting engagement in All India Radio, Madras. With an idea to take part in the Experts' deliberations at the Madras Music Academy and therefrom proceed to Tiruvaiyaru, Ramakrshnayya Pantulu started from Vijayawada. To provide an opportunity to his young disciple to listen to great masters of music at Tiruvaiyaru, he took Pattabhiramayya and Balamuralikrshna with him. After the Academy's sessions were over, as also, Murali's engagement, all of them came to Tiruvaiyaru.

Pantulu felt greatly elated to observe how one single song by his young disciple secured him accolades from great stalwarts of music. He thought that the boy was a Divine incarnation and it was only his own fortune to have him as his disciple. He firmly believed that Tyagaraja, who wanted that the concept, '*nadopasana* is the easy way to God-realisation', should reach all, has reborn in the form of this boy, to fulfil his desire. He approached the organisers and requested them to give his ward a programme, in lieu of his own, slated on 7.1.1942. The organisers were a bit hesitant, whether a boy of such a young age, would be able to enrapture the listeners for a full one hour. But they consented to provide only thirty minutes to the boy keeping in mind the overwhelming enthusiasm of the public. Is it not a great thing to get thirty minutes, at that peak time, when it is difficult to get a chance to sing even a single *kriti*? What else could a *guru* aspire when there is a disciple, who could win a great name for his *guru*?

The whole village of Tiruvaiyaru reverberated with the words, "Some one from Andhra; we are not sure whether he would be ten or less; those who heard him during the *aradhana* say that he is Tyagaraja re-born. Today at 5 p.m. his programme has been announced; we must reach the pandal and occupy a seat at vantage point, well in advance". The time approached and the crowd was anxiously looking around for the boy's arrival. The hissing noise, arising out of the secret conversations between the people appeared to be the roars of sea waves. First, the accompanying artistes came and sat on the platform. A volunteer brought Balamuralikrshna and placed him at the centre of the platform. Those who had not seen him already were surprised. Is this, that boy? May not be more than ten. How is it that everyone says that he is an incarnation? To have a closer look at him, the crowd, sitting in the back rows, started to move forward. So, the organisers brought a wooden box and made it the seat for the young boy. Pattabhiramayya, with the *Tambura*, set behind Balamurali. The boy folded his hands, paying respects to the idol of Tyagaraja and then to his *guru*, started to sing, with a smile curling on his lips. Nobody could realise, at the outset, that he has commenced, for his voice was in perfect alignment with the pitch. The next moment, pin drop silence prevailed everywhere. Raga Alapana, followed by *kritis* and *swaraprastara* came in succession. The listeners felt that they were drinking the elixir of nectar. They wondered: What is the meaning of a constant smile on his lips? Is it the symbol of flowering of a soul-stirring art? Is it the reflection of great confidence, acquired through proficiency? Music is said to be an art, one could get after many lives and by vigorous practice for a length of time, but, this boy seems to have got it at this tender age! Or could it be due to his having got the privileged time slot, to sing in that holy place and having great musicians in the audience? Thoughts in this manner were reeling in the minds of the people, while the hands of the clock also moved fast, as it seemed. Only thirty minutes time was allotted to him, though nobody was conscious that he had already crossed the fortysixth minute. On and on the boy continued to sing even as the organisers stood tongue-tied and amazed at the magnificent recital. It was as if everyone was released from the bonds of *Brahmastra*, when the programme came to an end. The whole crowd stood up as if the day's programmes were over and rushed towards the platform. Exactly at that time, a volunteer came and lifted the young Balamurali and disappeared in the crowd. Inspite of the organiser's announcement, that the boy was already exhausted and they would arrange the next day, for the boy's presence there, so that people could see him closer and know about him, to maintain order was a difficult process. Pattabhiramayya and Pantulu were perturbed as to what happened to the boy, but they were happy to get the information that Murali was safe with Bangalore Nagaratnamma and they went there.

Nagaratnamma knew that when enthusiasm and anxiety cross the limit, the masses would become hysterical, which could cause harm to young Murali and so she had sent a volunteer to bring him to her room. She called in a saint, who was passing by her room and prayed to him, with the words, "*Swami!* Did you listen to this boy's divine music? Could there be any doubt that he is only our *Swami* (meaning Tyagaraja) reborn? Please bless him for a long life, to serve the cause of music. Evils should never affect this boy". The *Swamiji* asked for a coconut, rounded it above the head of Murali and broke it open. Putting his palm on the young singer's head, he uttered, "His birth is purposeful. Nobody can oppose him and he will never meet failure in his artistic life" and presented Murali a small garland of *tulasi* beads.

Next day, the people who came in multitudes to see the boy were disappointed, since Pantulu and Pattabhiramayya, after taking leave from Nagaratnamma, left the earlier night itself to Tanjavur, with Murali. A wealthy Chettiar from Arimazham, in Chettinadu, brought a silver vessel to be presented to Balamurali, but he had to send it through Daliparti Pichahari, a Nagaswara artiste of Andhra Pradesh and a disciple in vocal music of Parupalli Ramakrshnayya Pantulu. This was the first occasion in the history of the Tiruvaiyaru *aradhana* festival that a musician was presented a gift. The name and fame that Balamuralikrshna got at Tiruvaiyaru (and even after) was due to only Pantulu's blessings and affection, which Balamurali still cherishes in his heart with reverence. Tiruvaiyaru became the window to Balamurali's prowess and caused an introduction of this great artiste to Tamilnadu and many other states.

It is quite common among the people of Andhra Pradesh to say proudly that Balamurali belongs to their state or district. At the same time, those from Tamilnadu, Karnataka and Kerala also shower on him their affection as the greatest musician of the century. There are some who claim that they are the relatives or intimate friends of Balamurali. It is not a matter of surprise, many young musicians deem him (many openly announce) as their *guru*. In fact, he might have been born in Andhra, domiciled in Tamilnadu, given numberless concerts not only in Karnataka and Kerala, but throughout the length and breadth of the country. It would not be an exaggeration, if we say that he incarnated in this country as an outcome of India's cultural penance and as such he is the whole Nation's property. Normally, writing biographies of great personages is done only after their time which may, at times, give room to errors or fabrications of truth. It is only my good fortune — a dust of my *guru's* feet — to put in words, the biography of my revered *guru*, the Collossus of Music, Dr. Balamuralikrshna.

Nature wanted him to come on the earth, in a human form, and he has come. But, some of his elder relatives, lamented on the sixteenth day of his appearance on this earth, "Why was he born?" In fact, many would have felt happy, if he had left this world, on the day of his birth itself. Poor ones! They didn't know then that only this seed would sprout as a great banyan tree, making everyone of his relatives and friends — even the state of his birth — proud and happy, by becoming the uncrowned monarch of the world of Carnatic music.

So far, we witnessed him at Tiruvaiyaru. We have aligned with the pitch. Shall we align our voice with that and enjoy the Splendour of *Swaras*?

Roaming with a Wild Thirst

Balamuralikrshna hails from a family which considered music as on 'outcaste' thing: Before going into details about this maestro and his artistic achievements, it is necessary to know about his father, Pattabhiramayya, who was the first in that family to take to music. The travails and tribulations he had to undergo in this process was heart-rending and it is a story which would help to understand his son's background.

Music was generally a taboo, particularly among the orthodox brahmin caste. Antarvedipalem is a tiny hamlet in the Rajole Taluk of west Godavari district in Andhra Pradesh. There lived Venkataramayya, a Teluganya brahmin, with the family name, Mangalampalli. Mangalampalli may be the name of the place to which his ancestors belonged, though, today no village with that name is traceable. Venkataramayya was a scholar in *vedas* and *sastras* and served as a *purohit* to the Kshatriya families, who lived in and around the village. Everyone respected him very much and his word was taken as that of a divine person. His wife, Seetamma was an embodiment of tolerance and pious virtues. In the course of time, this couple got thirteen children — ten boys and three girls.

Pattabhiramayya was born on 17.9.1892 as the sixth

child and fourth among the male children. He was named after Venkataramayya's maternal uncle. The senior Pattabhiramayya's wife, Chalamamma was very affectionate to the junior and since she could not address him with the name of her husband, as was the custom, she christened the boy with a pet name, 'Kazulu'. There were and still are, many south Indian ladies, who never pronounce their husband's name. In the fifth year, Pattabhiramayya was put in a school and the sacred thread was given to him when he was eight. According to the convention that one would not teach his own son, Venkataramayya brought a *pandit* from somewhere, giving accommodation and food, put the boy under his care to do *adhyayana* of the sacred texts. The reason behind such a convention was that the parental affection would put a deterrent on discipline of the boy. The teacher within a few months, absconded after taking to saffron robes. Venkataramayya felt sorry that his son's *Vedic* learning got suspended, but it was a happy situation for Pattabhiramayya. He had no inclination or interest towards the orthodoxy or discipline. Perfunctorily he attended the school and somehow managed to reach the eighth standard. He commenced his lessons in Sanskrit from Krishnamacharyulu of the same village and then went to his second elder brother, Somanna, who was living in Sakhinetipalli, to learn Astrology. It is not known how he imbibed an interest in music, all these years. A flair for music dawned only on him in that family. He approached, in secrecy, a music teacher, Picchi Anantacharlu and started clandestine practice for some days. He knew very well that his musical desire was quite against the family's traditional orthodoxy. The musicians in those days (there were some brahmins too) were considered as 'untouchables' and most of them won their bread by accompanying the dancers, performing behind them. Venkataramayya passed away in 1903, leaving the family's burden on his wife and on the eldest son, Seetaramayya.

Though the loss of his father was grief to Pattabhiramayya, he need not thereafter worry about the disciplinarian-cum always punishing father. But, now it was the turn of Seetaramayya to worry about this brother of his. The young fellow did not stick to one particular thing and was quite irregular in everything he attempted to do. One day Seetaramayya got angry. Throwing a brass pot on his brother, he shouted, "You unlucky fellow! Enough of being a burden here. You may choose your own way of life. Get lost and don't turn back". Venkataratna Sastri, younger brother of Venkataramayya, was a great philosopher and a devotee of the Divine. He was the *asthana puranic* expositor in the *zamin* of Alluri Pedda Suryanarayana Rao of Chintalapalli, near Antarvedipalem. After a word with his mother, Seetaramayya sent his brother, Pattabhiramayya, to Chintalapalli, so that the boy could learn one or two lessons in Sanskrit from uncle Sastri. *Bhajans* were almost a daily ritual in the *zamin* and naturally, they attracted Pattabhiramayya more than anything else. Soon, he learnt to sing some *Adhyatma Ramayana Keertanas, Gopika Geeta* and so on. After all that, he learnt only few chapters in Kalidasa's *Raghuvamsa* from Sastri. In Datipaka, a village close by Chintalapalli, lived a musician, by name, Kocharlakota Rama Raju and he was a composer too. He was a violinist and a left-hander (bowing on the instrument with his left hand). Having heard about him, Pattabhirammyya, without telling anybody at home, left for Detipaka. The boy's disappearance brought great anguish to Venkataratna Sastri. With the help of the *zamindar*, he sent many servants of the *zamin* to various places in search of the boy. Venkataratna Sastri worried that the responsibility entrusted to him by his sister-in-law could not be taken care of. Surprisingly, Pattabhiramayya himself returned on the sixth day and when asked, he narrated everything but added that since Rama Raju's method of teaching music didn't suit him, he decided to return. The truth was something else. Coming to know that the boy belonged to Venkataratna Sastri's family and that he had come without anybody's knowledge, Rama Raju himself had sent him back, escorted by some of his disciples. One day the *zamindar* asked Pattabhiramayya "What man!

How is it that you do not show any respect to your uncle? Without learning Sanskrit from him, do you want to learn music, which is undesirable to your family? Are you going to put *tala* at the back of prostitutes?" Pattabhiramayya didn't reply, though his mind was engaged in searching for another music teacher. Few months later, in 1906, Sastri fell a prey to the cholera epidemic and Pattabhiramayya had return to Antarvedipalem. The elders in the family were immersed in the thought as to what this bohemian would do in the future for his livelihood.

Bhagavatula Papayya Sastri was Pattabhiramayya's paternal aunt's son and the husband of his eldest sister. He was a man with rich worldly knowledge, inspite of being a *Vedic* scholar. During one of his visits to Antarvedipalem, Seetamma lamented to him about her son. Sastri said that one could make a name, if only encouraged in what he wants to do and in Pattabhiramayya's case, it would be better if he were allowed to learn music. He also clarified the wrong notion that learning music meant that one should only go after dancers, to win the bread. Nobody could say 'no', when the proposal came from the eldest son-in-law. Pattabhiramayya was sent with Papayya Sastri.

Bhagavatula Venappa, maternal uncle of Pattabhiramayya lived in the village, Elamanchili, of the Narasapur Taluk and in the same village was a music teacher, by name, Subramania Iyer. This Subramania Iyer belonged to Tamilnadu and came to Elamanchili, to train some aspiring youngsters, in music. Staying in Venappa's house, Pattabhiramayya started his musical lessons under Subramania Iyer. He spent most of the time only with the *guru* and became a favourite student amongst others. The family members, either in Antarvedipalem or Elamanchili were really not happy over the boy's aptitude for music, but were contented that at least now he had found out a track. But this contentment did not last long. After about five months, Subramania Iyer started out saying that he would come back in a day or two, after finishing his urgent work at Palacole. The *chela* also followed and the teacher desisted. Finally, Subramania Iyer had to give in because the student hung on. Thereafter there was no news about both of them for quite some time. Once again sobs and laments were heard in the families of Antervedipalem and Elamanchili. By the way, nobody knew who this Subramania Iyer was and wherefrom he came. A report to the Police would only become adverse, for they could not attend the laborious questioning sessions, frequently. One day a letter came from Subramania Iyer, in which he had stated that he had to rush to his native place, Pakshiteertham, situated in the Chingleput district of Tamilnadu, on some urgent work and Pattabhiramayya had also accompanied him on the trip, adamantly.

Pattabhiramayya had compelled his teacher to take him also, only with the idea that opportunities would be more of learning, if he stayed with the teacher, constantly. Pakshiteertham was not a bed of roses to Subramania Iyer. Because he had incurred heavy debts there, got as hand loans or as advance for taking music lessons, he left for Andhra Pradesh shifting from place to place there. Now he had come back, only with the thought that the interval of fifteen years would have wiped out the memories of his earlier misdeeds and he was right. All the money he had earned so far, had run out and it was very difficult to get fresh tutions. He had a friend — a Gujerati brahmin - who earlier worked in the temple as a cook and now was on the same job but at Kancheepuram. When these friends met, they discussed the prospects Iyer could get at Kancheepuram and it is needless to say that Pattabhiramayya also followed. The latter's travails started only there. The intimacy between Tawker, the Gujerati and Iyer proportionately diluted the relationship between the teacher and the student. Tawker mischievously used to accuse Pattabhiramayya of this or that mistake and finally the lad from Andhra was thrown out. Pattabhiramayya had to spend that night on the *pial* of a *chaultry* and the next morning when went to the adjacent Kumara Kottam temple, the cook of that temple, out of pity brought and offered him some *prasadams*. He also helped Pattabhiramayya to write a letter to Antarvedipalem, stating that he was cheated by the teacher, whom he trusted so much and if some money was sent, he would proceed to Tanjavur, the capital of Carnatic music, for regular coaching there.

In fact, his relatives were worrying whether the desultory boy was alive or not, since the letters posted to Pakshiteertham returned undelivered. The letter from his brother made Seetaramayya happy and he sent some money. He also had advised his brother to come back, since their mother was unwell and the boy could later go to Thanjavur and pursue his musical studies. Pattabhiramayya, as per his brother's letter, started for home and he had to spend the night on the Railway platform at Madras. In the wee hours he woke up only to see a big stone placed as pillow beneath is head, where he kept his baggage. He ran here and there and accosted a police Inspector, who luckily was a Telugu speaking man. Seeing the plight of Pattabhiramayya, he managed to find out the thief and retrieved the bag. Pattabhiramayya finally boarded the train that steamed to his native place.

The return of this 'adventurer' made everyone happy. One day, Papayya Sastri came to Antarvedipalem and conversed with Pattabhiramayya. He said, "I am reminded of something which your uncle Venkataratna Sastri told me, when I was a student under him, learning Sanskrit. He had his training in Pedda Kallepalli, a village in the Krshna district, where lives a great *vidwan*, Susarla Dakshinamurthi Sastri, who is in a way, a distant relative of ours. He is not only a scholar in Sanskrit but highly proficient in music also, having learnt from Venkatasubbayya, the cousin and disciple of Sri Tyagaraja. Many come to him to learn music. In view of his children's higher education, he has shifted to, and now lives in Machilipatnam. He is a very kind hearted person and it would be difficult to find such a one among our relatives. If I take you to him, would you be regular in taking lessons from him?" Pattabhiramayya gave a thought, for sometime, to the hardships he underwent sometime back and then gave his consent. Parting with the tear-eyed mother once again, Pattabhiramayya started for Machilipatnam.

Susarla Dakshinamurthi Sastri of Pedda Kallepalli (also called 'Dakshina Kasi' and 'Kadaleepuram') was born on 1-7-1860, as the son of Susarla Gangadhara Sastri (senior) and Lakshmamma. At the age of 17, he went to Tanjavur and learnt music for five years from Manambucchavadi Venkatasubbayya. This Venkatasubbayya, son of the paternal aunt of Tyagaraja was also the first disciple of the Saint composer. Returning to his native village, Dakshinamurthi Sastri began to teach music free to aspiring students, also providing them free boarding and lodging. "Gayaka Sarvabhouma" Parupalli Ramakrshnayya Pantulu was one among Sastri's eminent disciples. Dakshinamurthi Sastri passed away on 30-7-1917.

Although Pattabhiramayya had learnt few *Geetas* from Pakshiteertham Subramania Iyer, Sastri now started again with *Geetas*. The *Guru* used to explain and clarify all the doubts of his students, patiently. After lunch, he would relax on an easy-chair and teach compositions, with the students sitting around. Two or three time he would sing a line of some *kriti* and enter into a short nap. The students would go on repeating the line taught. Sastri would wake up after about two or three minutes and would go for the next *sangati* (embellishment). He was keeping ten resident students in Pedda Kallepalli and now, at Machilipatnam, there were only five. He could not afford to keep more. Pattabhiramayya did not want to give any additional trouble to his *guru*. He used to go to few houses and had his supper in any one of them, by turn. Sometimes, he felt glad to think that 'Starvation is the best medicine'!

Mangalampalli Pedda Raghavulu was a native of Elamanchili. His daughter, Seetamma, lived in Machilipatnam with her husband, Gudur Rangasayee, a Revenue Inspector. Pattabhiramayya had close acquaintance with that family and used to frequent their house. Rangasayee requested Pattabhiramayya to teach music to his two daughters (through his first wife) and in return the teacher could have his food in his house. This arrangement was greatly helpful to Pattabhiramayya.

Susarla Gangadhara Sastri (junior), brother's son of Dakshinamurthi Sastri learnt music from his uncle and lived in Machilipatnam. He became a flute player and was a good friend of Pattabhiramayya. Soon Pattabhiramayya, with the permission of Dakshinamurthi Sastri, commenced to learn music from Gangadhara Sastri also. Whenever Sastri practised on the flute, Pattabhiramayya would sit with the *Sruti*-box. This keen observations evoked an interest in the latter to try his hand on the flute. Dakshinamurthi Sastri taught him only vocal music and Violin playing. Gangadhara Sastri guided Pattabhiramayya in handling the flute deftly.

However great one's musical talent may be, it was a custom to go to Tamilnadu, to win the approval and appreciation of the *vidwans* of that state and also to acquaint with the *bani* (style) of the 'Kaveri delta'. So also, Gangadhara Sastri undertook a journey to Thanjavur to develop his own musical potential and Pattabhiramayya also joined him. During the sojourn, they had the opportunity to meet one day, the famous flutist, Sarabha Sastri, who was a *sahadhyayi* of Dakshinamurthi Sastri. Some months later, they returned to Machilipatnam, where Pattabhiramayya got few more tutions and one or two performing opportunities.

Once Pattabhiramayya had gone to Eluru for a flute performance, at the request of some of his friends. A lady in the audience, at the end of the programme, came near Pattabhiramayya, gave her address and requested him to positively meet her, the next day. Hoping that she had invited him only to present some compliments, as a token of her appreciation, Pattabhiramayya met her, as requested. There was no present waiting for him, but, on the other hand, he was offered a job! The lady was born blind and had her training in the Braille system, at Bombay. She possessed an extra-ordinary talent in solving any difficult problem in Mathematics. Utilising this, she had started to conduct 'Mathematical-feat' shows and would mesmerize the assemblage with her solutions, at the spur of a moment. These shows fetched good collection, wherever she conducted them. At the same time, she had a handicap. She required music from a Harmonium or any other instrument, to stimulate her brain. For this purpose, she carried a small Harmonium and played herself, but found it difficult to do both simultaneously and was looking for someone who could help with the music part. This was the job offered to Pattabhiramayya and the lady assured to look after the boarding and lodging, besides a nominal amount as monthly salary. Her story so moved Pattabhiramayya that he readily accepted the offer. Six performances in a period of fifteen days were held, but, Pattabhiramayya did not want to continue and so asked the lady to release him, but she turned down the request. One day, after informing her that he would return after visiting a local 'brother', he flew away. On his way to Antarvedipalem, he alighted at Narasapur to meet his friend, Rangachari. After releasing a laugh on hearing the story of the lady, Rangachari said, "In fact I was about to send you a message, but luckily, you have yourself come. This is the matter. I have been appointed as the palace *vidwan* in the *zamin* of Mandasa (Visakhapatnam district). The *zamindar* wants to get his son trained on the flute by some good teacher. I hope you won't have any objection to take up this assignment". The words *Asthana*, 'Palace' and *Zamin* pushed Pattabhiramayya to great heights and so he started with Rangachari, after about four days. They stayed in a *chaultry* and it took twentyfive days to have an audience with the *zamindar*. Rangachari gave violin performance, with Pattabhiramayya on the flute. The *zamindar* was pleased enough to appoint the new flute teacher. The young *zamindar* would sit only for five or ten minutes, learn one line and say to his teacher, "Alright! you may now go. I shall send for you, after some days, when I finish practicing this". Pattabhiramayya never expected such a mode of teaching or learning, which annoyed him. So, taking leave of Rangachari, who offered twenty five rupees for the expenses, he came to the railway station. While waiting for the train's arrival Pattabirammayya thought, "Having come such a long distance, why not I visit that place?" — and bought a ticket to Calcutta. On board the train, a Telugu speaking old man was sitting opposite to Pattabhiramayya. Making acquaintance with him, he understood that the old man was also bound for Calcutta. The old man acted as a guide to Pattabhiramayya, at Calcutta, showing him many places, temples and other memorials. When both of them reached back to the railway station, Pattabhiramayya asked the other, "Now, where are we going?", to which "Kasi" was the reply. Ah! Kasi! The most sacred place! The holy river Ganga flows there and on its banks is situated the temple of Lord Viswanatha. Did not Seetaramayya set out on pilgrimage to Kasi, about ten years ago and extol the whole story over a period of six months? It would only be a sin if Kasi was not visited. Thinking on these lines, Pattabhiramayya requested the old man to take him also to Kasi. When they reached Kasi, the old man thought "What an inconvenience even coming to Kasi?" and decided to part from the 'parasite' — like Pattabhiramayya. He, saying, "This is Kasi.... Go ahead", disappeared. Where and how to go? He was reminded of Varahagiri Narayana Rao, in whose house Seetaramayya stayed during his trip. The *tongawalla* demanded six rupees to take Pattabhiramayya to Hanuman Ghat, but he had only one and half rupee. He had no other go but to walk the distance and after great difficulty, he found out the house of Narayana Rao. Coming to know that a member belonging to the Mangalamalli family had come, Narayana Rao extended his hospitality by providing food and accommodation for two days. Later Pattabhiramayya had to go to various *Dharmasalas* for food and thus spent twentyfive days. He again wrote to his brother, Seetaramayya to send some money, care of Narayana Rao. The brother immediately responded by sending money with a piece of instruction to stay out of Antarvedipalem, since the police was on the look out for him, on a complaint lodged by some blind lady. Without worrying about all this, Pattabhiramayya came straight to Antarvedipalem. In the meantime, his sister's husband Kamanna and brother, Jagannatham had a talk with the police and had managed to drop the case.

After about a fortnight's time, Pattabhiramayya returned to Machilipatnam. Gangadhara Sastri had already shifted his residence to Vijayawada, which would make it convenient for him to undertake journeys easily. Coming to know of this Pattabhiramayya also migrated to Vijayawada.

Settlement in Vijayawada brought prosperity to Pattabhiramayya. Number of aspiring students came to Gangadhara Sastri to learn music, but since he could not undertake all, he directed many to Pattabhiramayya. Seetamma and Seetaramayya felt extremely happy that Pattabhiramayya was now able to send them some money, after making proviso of his own maintenance. People came from many quarters to Seetaramayya seeking marital alliance with Seetaramayya's family. He also decided to get his brother, Pattabhiramayya married and consultation of many horoscopes went negative. Finally one was selected. It was that of Sooryakantamma, daughter of Prayaga Rangayya of Gudimellanka, a village in Rajole taluk. Rangayya was a prolific composer and Dr. B. Rajanikanta Rao has spoken highly of him in his history of the great composers of Andhra ("Andhra Vaggeyakara Charitamu"). Few months after the betrothal, the wedding of Pattabhiramayya and Sooryakantamma was celebrated. In 1918, Sooryakantamma was only nine years. Because of this, even after the marriage, she stayed with her parents for about eight years and came to Vijayawada only in 1926, to live with her husband. She was not educated in the modern sense of the term, but possessed sound knowledge in Telugu and Sanskrit, through home-study. In the course of time she learnt and became considerably proficient in Hindi also. Above all, she had more liking towards music. Music was her very life. Only due to this reason, Rangayya came forward to give her in marriage to Pattabhiramayya. Seetamma came to Vijayawada to see how her new daughters-in-law looked after the household. After few days, she returned to Antarvedipalem. Happy over her son's settled life, she breathed her last, at the age of sixty.

It was pleasant surprise to Pattabhiramayya when he came to know about Sooryakantamma's liking for music, the art to acquire which, he all along led a vagabond life. He wanted to coach her on the *veena* and procured an instrument through one Kuttachari and started the Primary lessons himself. Being not much competent to teach further, he shifted his residence to Gudiwada and engaged a good *veena* instructor. Within few months, by her ardent practice, Sooryakantamma acquired the ability to give concerts on that instrument. She was much devoted to Gandhian principles and spent her leisure in spinning on a *charka* (spindle). She took a vow to wear only *Khadi* all her life. At times, she would go on singing patriotic songs for hours. One of her daily prayers to God was that our country should be freed from the clutches of the British rule. Pattabhiramayya shifted back to Vijayawada after some time.

Four years passed. Sooryakantamma became pregnant. In the eighth month of pregnancy, she was invited by her parents and other elders to come to Sankaraguptam, a village, where the Prayaga family was then living. She did not want to move out of Vijayawada, for she did not want to abandon her musical practice. But the prevailing custom compelled her to go to her parent's house. On her way, she went first to Antarvedipalem and had to extend her stay there, because her uncle, Srinivasa Rao passed away in the village and she could not go there, until the pollution caused by his death got purified.

Normally, any lady would become very happy, on her pregnancy, that too for the first time. Contrary to this, Sooryakantamma became worried. During her confinement she would be deprived of continuing her musical practice. In Sankaraguptam, she was not allowed to do any work and so she spent most of the time in playing on the *veena*, which she had carefully brought with her. The native doctor advised her rest but she felt that music and herself were inseparable and so she did not stop her practice. She made up her mind to leave the baby, after delivery, to her elder sister, Subbamma and devote her own time to music. Labour pains started on 5 July and the next evening, she gave birth to a male child.

Sooryakantamma showered all her love and affection on the infant, born on 6 July, 1930. Sometimes she would place her mouth on his ears, as if revealing some secret, at which act, the relatives and neighbours would simply laugh. On the thirteenth day she had mild headache, followed by fever and the thermometer went on rising. Native doctors were rushed in and an English doctor from a nearby town was also sent for. Pattabhiramayya hurried from his own village to Sankaraguptam and stuck to the bedside of his wife. Sooryakantamma regained consciousness on the third day and at about ten p.m. she called her sister, Subbamma and asked for some water. Subbamma poured few drops in her mouth. Next moment, the swan set to sail. Pattabhiramayya ran out crying; he felt a dense darkness was ahead of him. Obsequies were duly performed to the departed soul. Some elders in the family and village people cursed the new born. "Sinful fellow! He came only to swallow his mother. Soorya would have lived for many more years, had this child not been born". Many of them were hundred per cent sure that this sixteen day old infant would also not survive. How could they know that this boy would live a long life and become great in the field of music and his very name, Balamuralikrshna, was going to be a craze among the music lovers? But out of all others there was one who loved the child more affectionately than even his mother. It was Subbamma.

Subbamma, elder sister of Sooryakantamma, lost her husband in about a fortnight's time, after her marriage. At the age of seven, she returned as a widow to her parent's house and continued living there. Till her end, she did not know what worldly life was and she was more like a saint. She had no responsibility or worry of any kind all these years. Now, God had entrusted to her the liability to rear up her sister's son, nay, her own son from that moment. Sooryakantamma once had called Subbamma and opened her heart: "Sister! I am going to thrust on your shoulders the burden of bringing up my child, from the day it is born. I cannot devote time on it hampering my music. So, it is for you to lookafter the child". Subbamma brushed away these words as unimportant, coming out of one, who evinced excessive interest in music. She had not even thought of that it would come true, so soon.

Pattabhiramayya got ready to start, after a fortnight's stay in the house of his in-laws. He was stuffing his wife's jewels and some other articles in a bag, which annoyed many ladies of the house. "Oh! you have decided to cut off our relationship. When you are careful to take away with you, all these articles of your wife, why should you leave your son here? What is the necessity for us to look after the child? Take him also with you" - shouted they. On hearing these words, Subbamma came out the kitchen and chided them: "Do you have any sense? Why are you raucous? He is already grief struck, by the loss of his wife. Why do you prick his heart? Our girl is no more, then why do we require her jewels and other things? Many would be ready to give him their daughter. Don't you remember the words of his eldest brother, Seetaramayya, the other day? But because of this child, many are in the queue with the proposal for alliance. Let this child not be a hindrance to his father's re-marriage. I am this boy's mother and am going to keep him with me, come what may. I shall get the pleasure of seeing Soorya in the face of this boy. Look here, Pattabhiramayya! Don't think I am saying this to manage the present situation. Even before her confinement, your wife had ordained me to take the responsibility of this child. I swear in the name of God, I shall lookafter your son, carefully, to the best of my abilities. Discard all your worries about the child. You may happily go away now. If you feel, you can come here to see the boy, whenever you want". So saying, she went in with the child.

Vijayawada appeared to Pattabhiramayya as a dense forest, where he had been exiled. Who was there to enquire about his welfare? It was not a house to him, but a haunted place. Sweet concords of music that reverberated there from the *veena* and the voice of his dear wife now became extinct. Mechanically, he resumed his tutions. It was certain that the distress in his heart would fade out, if only his boy was also there. But how to take care of him? Marrying again, as proposed by his brothers, would in no way help, for in many such cases, only the child became the victim. He wiped out of his heart the thought of any personal pleasure; he should never marry again and must live all alone, with the sole aim to bring up his only son. That would be enough for him in the remaining years of life.

The boy was lying on the laps of Subbamma. Patting on his back softly, she was remonstrating: "If your mother were alive, you need not lie on the lap of this unlucky woman. People may curse you, hate you. If only God's grace is there, you will certainly become a great man and smear coal on their faces. But, I do not know whether I will live to see you becoming great". She was now a Yasoda, who brought up Krshna, the son of Devaki. She named the boy as Kṛshna, but used to call him Murali, a pet name. Perhaps Subbamma might have had foresight to know that this boy would reign the whole world of Music, like Lord Krshna, who enraptured the universe by his magic flute and fittingly named him after the divinity. During later conversation, she explained, "Then I didn't know Murali would become a great musician, It was only his mother's wish that if the child is a male, he should be named 'Krshna' and I simply carried it out, that's all. Maybe, his mother administered music in his ears by keeping her mouth on them, often. But, I fed him with baby food, branded 'Milkmaid'".

Pattabhiramayya once went to Eluru, on some work.

A friend of his informed that Subbamma was there and staying with her brother, Prayaga Lakshmana Sastri. As soon as Pattabhiramayya stepped in through the door, Krshna as if recognizing him, got onto his shoulders. Welcoming her brother-in-law, Subbamma exclaimed: "See this. The fellow has somehow known his father, got on to him and refuses to get down. Is this not consanguinity?" Next day, during the post-lunch chat, Pattabhiramayya disclosed his desire: "Life is unbearable to me without having a look at my son. I have determined not to marry again, for the boy's sake. Sister-in-law is a free bird. If she kindly agrees to come with the boy to Vijayawada and stay there , at least for some time, I would retrieve peace of mind. Whenever she wants, she may go wherever she likes. Please consider my state and do not refuse my request". Consultation between the sister and her brother consumed many hours. Lakshmana Sastri was in favour of Pattabhiramayya and Subbamma had no choice but to agree. She came to Vijayawada with Muralikrshna. Though she was his sister-in-law, Pattabhiramayya held her with high respect and considered her as another mother of his.

Every morning Pattabhiramayya would ride on a bicycle, taking young Murali in a attached bucket-seat, to the houses, where he took classes in music. The people there would fondly take the boy inside. The elders offered him milk and toffees while the youngsters played with him till Pattabhiramayya's classes were over. If for some reason, he did not bring Murali with him, they hung disappointed faces. Murali became a lovable child to everyone.

One day Pattabhiramayya went out alone and on his return, Subbamma complained to him: "See! I can do the household chores, if only this boy is away with you. Do you know what he did today? You once roamed from place to place, undergoing many difficulties to learn music, but this fellow, it seems, wants to acquire it at this age of two. As soon as you leave this place, he starts to meddle with the *tambura* and takes out the violin from the box. He does not look at the toys, which you brought for him. First of all, go and check up you musical instruments." Pattabhiramayya went inside the room where the musical instruments had been kept. No harm had been done to any of them. He felt extremely happy to know that his son evinced keen aptitude for music, even before he could speak legibly. Subbamma was faced with another regular problem. If at all Murali was to be fed, some students of Pattabhiramayya, available at that time, should sing until the boy's stomach was full. Music was the only trick to make Murali eat, without resistance.

Muralikrshna, now four, was regular to sit with his father's students and keenly watch their singing or playing. The seed of music had already been sowed in him by God, while he was in his mother's womb.

Rajolu was a place with many schools to teach English and other subjects. Pattabhiramayya thought, to give Murali a good education, it would be better to move over to that place. Many close relatives also lived there. But oncoming to know that opportunities for him to teach music and earn there were meager, he abandoned the idea. That was a time, when some musicians purchased plots for house construction in the locality now called, Satyanarayanapuram. Parupalli Ramakrshnayya Pantulu and Lanka Venkateswarlu were also among them. They suggested to Pattabhiramayya that it would only be proper to purchase one of his own and on their insistence. Pattabhiramayya managed to raise an amount of Rupees eight hundred only, being the cost of the site, measuring four hundred square yards. He erected a small thatched cottage on it. All along he was living in a *pucca* house, though rented, and now he had to adjust and compromise with the cottage. How could he think of brick house, having no penny in his pocket? He planned to sell half the land, with the help of which he could fulfil his desire. Just at that time, his elder brother, Somanna, an astrologer came from Sakhinetapilli, where he lived. He rebuked Pattabhiramayya for his silly idea, and after a thorough inspection of the site said: "This entire plot is very auspicious and would bring great fortune to you.

Whoever lives here would soon become very rich. Dont' mind, now you are not in position to construct a *pucca* house. This site has a power to get itself developed. You should on no account, sell even an inch of land". Sometime later, Pattabhiramayya's friends volunteered to help him financially. He removed the cottage and built a three-storeyed house and named it "Sooryakanta Bhavanam", after his wife and performed the *Grahapravesa* on 22.8.1937.

When Murali reached the eighth year, he diverted his attention more and more towards music. As soon as a *kriti* was sung by any of his father's students, he would start repeating the same, with more embellishments. Singing Kalpanaswaras could be mastered only after long practice and experience, but, in the case of this young boy, it was an ordinary affair. At times, he would execute them in three speeds of tempo. All this he did of his own, not tutored by anyone. Pattabhiramayya began to teach him *Geetas*, though Murali, by then, had memorised few *Varnas*. Days moved. Friends of Pattabhiramayya who were musicians, started to frequent his house every evening, to enjoy Murali's music. They would themselves provide accompaniments. Khambampati Akkaji Rao, a notable *veena* artiste and disciple of Pattabhiramayya and Mahadevu Radhakrshna Raju, an eminent *mrudangam vidwan* were among them. Pattabhiramayya was contemplating about a *guru*, under whose care Murali could be entrusted. After consulting some intimate friends, he decided that Parupalli Ramakrshnayya Pantulu would alone be the ideal *guru* to Balamurali.

Parupalli Ramakrshnayya Pantulu (5.12.1883/ 16.7.1951), the greatest among the musicians of Andhra, was a disciple of Susarla Dakshinamurthi Sastri, who again was the disciple of Manambuchavadi Venkata-subbayya, the cousin and first disciple of Sri Tyagaraja. After gaining proficiency in Vocal music and also the violin, Pantulu went to Tamilnadu and was richly benefitted by listening to the music of Ramanathapuram *Poochi* Srinivasa Iyengar, Madurai Pushpavanam Iyer, Tirukodikaval Krishnayyar, Malaikottai Govindaswami

Pillai and such other celebrities. Pantulu earned laurels and awards galore. Andhra Saraswata Parishad conferred on him the title "Gayaka Sarvabhouma" in 1931 and many other institutions honoured him with titles like "Bharati Teerthopadhyaya" and so on. With a big moustache on his face and turban on his head, he appeared like a king, and he was really a king among musicians of Andhra Pradesh. Pattabhiramayya himself had learnt under him for about four years, when Susarla was affected with senility. Thus, Pantulu was both a *gurubhai* and *guru* to him. He was living in Vemur, near Tenali and on the suggestion of Susarla Gangadhara Sastri, Pattabhiramayya prevailed upon Pantulu to settle down in Vijayawada, years back. It fell on the part of Pantulu to later suggest to Pattabhiramayya to purchase a 'house-site' in Sathyanarayanapurm. By this, they maintained a cordial relationship.

On an auspicious day, Pattabhiramayya took his son, Murali, to Pantulu and requested him to teach the boy. Pantulu, after casting a glance on the countenance of Murali, laughed and said: "The boy seems to be very puny; to practice music, one has to be sound in health. Why do you want to trouble him at this tender age? You may yourself teach him now and bring to me after some years. Further, it will be tedious for you to bring him here everyday and take him back". Pattabhiramayya submitted, "Being puny is his natural build. If I teach him myself, a discipline cannot be expected from the boy. You have to accept him and this is my ernest request". Pantulu, at last, agreed and asked Murali to sing something, whatever he knew. On hearing a *Geeta*, sung by Murali, Pantûlu said, "Your son has a very sweet voice and he is able to do some phrases, imaginatively. No doubt, he has a bright future... Okay... Let me commence with another *Geeta*". He brought a notebook, wrote the *Geeta* with notation and asked Murali to repeat what he taught. Muralikrshna became the assiduous disciple of Ramakrshnayya Pantulu.

Gamut Enlivened

Susarla Dakshinamurthi Sastri festival was regularly conducted in Vijayawada by Ramakrshnayya Pantulu and his band of disciples. The programmes were usually chalked out by Pantulu. Only seventeen days remained for the commencement of the festival in the year 1940. Pantulu had to go to his village in connection with some urgent work and hence entrusted the charge of arranging the programmes to his disciple, Netilakshminarayana. Radhakrshna Raju and Lanka Venkateswarlu spoke to Lakshminarayana to somehow include Murali's recital in the schedule. Pattabhiramayya was worried and contended that to perform in the festival one should be a seasoned artiste and after all, Murali was too young. Further how could he sing without the knowledge of Pantulu, who had taken Murali under his wings, only few days back? All his arguments were of no avail. The *patrika* carried the name of Muralikrshna for a programme on 18.07.1940, on the *Ashada Suddha Ekadasi Day*. This was a coincidence, for Murali was born ten years before on the same *Ashada Suddha Ekadasi Day*. Pattabhiramayya asked his son whether he could sing, without any fear in the festival. Murali replied that he could do well, provided the accompanists were Akkaji Rao *(veena)* and Radhakrshna Raju *(mrudangam)*. These two were more familiar to Murali.

Pantulu, on his return, was taken aback to see Murali's name in the programme schedule. He called Lakshminarayana and remarked, " What is this? Are you all playing? This son of Pattabhiramayya has started to learn music only recently from me. I am afraid, the standard of the festival would go down by this abecedarian, who has not even completed a *Geeta*". Lakshminarayana pacified his *guru* by convincing him with the suggestion that if the boy's rendering was poor, they could very well ask him to stop abruptly and commence the next programme by Masunoori Sooryanarayana Bhagavater. Moreover, the programme notices have already been circulated locally and dispatched to other places.

On 18 July, at eight in the morning, the accompanists got on to the stage. Muralikrshna paid obeisance to Pantulu, who was sitting aside on the platform. The *guru* blessed him, *Vijayee Bhava*. (sing without any fear) and himself carried and placed his new disciple at the center of the stage. The father strumming the *tambura*, Murali commenced with the varna 'Vanajakshiro' in the *raga kalyani*, in three speeds of tempo. Then came a crisp *alapana* of the *raga*, *Jaganmohini*, followed by the *kriti* 'Sobhillu Saptasware'. The entire crowd was at first thinking that this youngster would vacate after delivering few compositions. But Murali's music was a poser to all. "Do you want melody? it is born with me; Do you expect proficiency? it is abundant; *Sruti, swara, laya* — whatever it is — they are before me, at my beck and call". The allotted time of thirty minutes already lapsed and the concert was crossing the third hour! Nobody felt it and were as if floating in a dream. Was this Narada of *tamburu?* No, it must be only Goddess Sarasvati. The audience mentally wandered to solve this sort of a puzzle. The concluding item, Mangalam brought them back to the conscious world. Pantulu stood up to say a few words, customarily, but his voice choked. Tears rolling from his eyes, he rushed into an adjacent room, carrying Murali on his shoulders and started to weep, like a child. He kissed the boy profusely. Musunoori

Sooryanarayana Bhagavatar usurped Pantulu's role and gave a lecture about Murali's music, in the place of his Katha Kalakshepa.

"It is nothing but our good fortune to be present here and to listen to this mesmerising music of Pattabhiramayya's son. He is only ten. Incredible! In fact, we were taken on an excursion to the higher worlds, by this boy. This is an epoch-making performance in the history of music. When Pantulu *guru* came to know about this programme, he got worried that the standard of the festival would get diminished. I am happy to say now that it has been only enhanced, thousand times. Muralikrshna will surely earn name and fame, not only to his family not only for his *guru* Pantulugaru but also to the whole of our Andhradesa. He reminds us of the young Muralikrshna of Brundavan, who swept away the universe by his sweet music. As such, I feel this young Muralikrshna may henceforth be called "Balamuralikrshna". I hope all of you would agree......... Thank you for the approval by a thunderous applause. Thanks are due to Pattabhiramayya for having kindly allowed his son to perform today and also to those who were instrumental in scheduling this programme. I pray God to shower upon Balamuralikrshna, all riches, fame and a very long, purposeful life". Bhagavatar was thanked by the audience in the form of acclamation. From then on, Muralikrshna came to be known as Balamuralikrshna. Pantulu, after circumposing the boy's head with his hand took out a fillip from the fingers, an apotropaic act.

Cool breeze had started to set in. Pattabhiramayya was now not a 'good for nothing', but the father of the boy, adored as Goddess Sarasvati Herself. Only that music, which was considered fit merely for putting *tala* at the back of prostitutes, had now brought a spring in his life. The art which was a taboo in the family had entered it without anyone's initiative. The same child, which was ten years ago, cursed by the relatives as to have been born only to kill his mother, had turned out as a pride to the family. Pattabhiramayya was not a mere 'music teacher' now; he was the father of an incarnation.

Subbamma was so overwhelmed with joy that she could not control her tears. She ran here and there, without knowing what to do. The boy had proved that he was fit for the name, she had fondly bestowed. If only his mother, to whom music was the lifeforce, were alive! Would it be her soul that entered the boy and brought out such scintillating music? Otherwise how could this ten year old tiny tot win the accolades from stalwarts? Anyway, she was luckier than Yasoda.

Next day, Parupalli appeared to be taciturn, quite against his nature. He could not get out of the spell cast by Muralikrshna. Was it not his own good luck to have the boy as his disciple? So far, he had not taught Murali more than a *Geeta*. Pantulu's heart was a fathomless ocean of love. He still could not really comprehend that the boy could sing so well? Had Pattabhiramayya and Lakshminarayana duped him by not saying anything about the boy's skill? No! they would not have dared to tell him and must have waited for an opportunity to make him know, by himself. Anyway, Muralikrshna had come to him, in the same way as Swami Vivekananda to Ramakrshna Paramhamsa. What else did he require in this life? His thoughts were cut off, when he saw Pattabhiramayya and Murali standing in front of him, for the boy's class. Pantulu asked, "What Pattabhiramayya? Are you joking with me? That's why, you have brought him". Pattabhiramayya got agitated as to what would be the reason for such words. Apologetically, he submitted, "Kindly excuse me. I myself didn't expect it. In fact, I didn't give my consent for the boy's performance, without prior permission from you. I had to give way when they insisted, that too thinking he would sing only one or two *keertanas*, which he had heard my students sing. Once again I request you to excuse me". Pantulu laughed and said, "What is all this? Do you think I am worried over this? No! nobody could be more happy than me. Murali is my pride, my honor, everything. Don't worry.

Enough of the *Geetas;* I shall start teaching him *keertanas*". The lessons ensued.

Muralikrshna would not go to his *guru's* house, everyday, as in the case of others. Once in three or four days, he would be there, Only when the *guru* sensed that the boy was in a mood to learn, he would sit and teach. On other days, Murali would roam in the streets on a small bicycle, which his father had newly purchased for him. The *guru,* in his classes, would first explain the meaning and mood of any song taken up and then start singing the first few lines. In the next class, Murali would do it perfectly well and they would move over. Very soon, Pantulu became deeply attatched and to spend a day without seeing Balamurali, only gave him restlessness. He would send for the boy. Keeping him either on his own lap or by his side, he would go on explaining the methods adopted for practice, grammar of music and so on. Balamurali gradually learnt about eight hundred *keertanas* from Parupalli Ramakrshnayya Pantulu, in about a dozen years.

After his debut in the Susarla Dakshinamurthi Sastri festival, Balamurali gave the next performance on 9.10.1940, during the Desara festival, held in the Durga Malleeswara temple of Durgapuram, a locality in Vijayawada. Eminent poets like Kasi Krshnacharyulu and 'Satavadhani' Chellailla Venkata Sastri were in the audience. At the close of the concert, Venkata Sastri, then and there, composed a verse in Telugu, praising Balamuralikrshna:

"Navalene Vruddhudavai
Navalene Keertiganchi
Navalene Sreedevi Sadbhaktudavai
Bhoovalayamu tirugumoyi Muralikrshna!"

(Live for innumerable years; earn unmeasurable fame; being a good devotee of the Goddess, come around the globe Muralikrshna).*

Bethapudi Sarbhayya, who renovated that temple

* Translated by the author from the original

and was a man with a noble heart, presented Balamurali with a golden laced velvet apparel.

The third concert was under the auspices of Ganakala Poushaka Sabha, Vijayawada. Next one on 30.11.1940 was his first out-of-town concert. It was in Machilipatnam. Earlier, Susarla Dakshinamurthi Sastri had also lived in this place. Harinagabhushanam Pantulu of Machilipatnam was a notable musician, but a lawyer by profession. He was the founder and the king-pin of the "Gana Vidyabhivardhani Sabha". Coming to know about Balamurali's memorable performance in the Tyagaraja festival in Vijayawada, through a saint named Vimalananda Bharati, Pantulu arranged the programme.

The concert began with a drizzle of honey. Many in the audience, every now and then were looking at Harinagabhushanam, to observe his mode of appreciation. Few minutes passed and Harinagabhushanam made an exit from the hall. Others thought that the boy's music was not upto the mark, as expected and that is why, he left the auditorium. But to everybody's surprise, Harinagabhushanam re-entered the hall, now with his family members. When the concert came to an end, he presented a gold medal to Balamurali and embraced him. Vimalananda Bharati stood up from among the audience and commended Murali, presenting another gold medal.

Balamurali's fame spread to all corners of the state and invitations started to come aplenty. Pattabhiramayya could not accept all and in many cases, he regretted simply by replying that the boy had become very weak and exhausted. He had to be selective. In the beginning albeit only gold and silver medals came in. Gradually Balamurali was given cash remuneration also. But that alone was not important.

Pattabhiramayya wanted to put his son in some school, when the boy attained his fifth year. Is it not important to have academic education also? But he had to postpone the idea, since the boy evinced no interest at all in attending any school. Most of the time he spent in playing with friends. Now, he had had started to give music performances and it was high time to admit him to any school. One day, the father took his son to the Municipal branch School, situated in a nearby locality, Buckimhampet and met the Headmaster. The latter conducted a test, by asking Murali to write a few words in Telugu, which the boy did, since he had learnt, at home to write one or two words. Satisfied with this, the Headmaster admitted him, straightaway, in the First Form (sixth standard). Every working day, in the mornings, there would be a prayer assembly, before the commencement of the classes. Every student, by turn, would render the prayer. When Murali's turn came, the Headmaster asked him to go ahead with a few more songs. This became a regular feature and the prayer assembly turned into a concert session and would continue till the bell rung for lunch break! There was a mathcmatics teacher in that school, who was of the staunch view that music is one to create havoc among mankind. He naturally became averse to Murali. Few months later, he met the Headmaster and said: "Sir! I don't think, this is good! Are we running an educational institution or conducting music concerts? In the quarterly examinations, all the students have secured only zero. Many parents are not happy over this and complain to me. If this goes on like this, what would be the standard of our school and how could we answer the parents, as well as the officials of our department?". One day, Puttaparti Narayanacharyulu, the Headmaster of the Municipal School, came to Pattabhiramayya. In the course of the conversation he said, "Why do you waste the boy's talent, in the name of schooling? Even highly educated boys are not able to get good jobs, except a clerk's post. Your son is, no doubt, an incarnation of Goddess Sarasvati. Art is one which could not be got so easily; one has to take many lives. You don't worry. English education could be got whenever one wants. There won't be any difficulty, if we engage a teacher to coach him, in your house itself. Did you notice his enthusiasm, when he goes to the house of Ramakrshnayya Pantulu? If you put a barricade to his art, it may cause detriment to his future life and at the same time, it will be an irreparable loss to the world of music. Think it over. You should pave way for his development in music than compelling him to pursue schooling". Ramakrshnayya Pantulu also said the same, when Pattabhiramayya sought his wise counsel, the next day. Pattabhiramayya pondered over. It is true even educated people do not get lucrative jobs. The boy, at the same time, has an enormous talent in music and no doubt, the fire is to be kindled. But, what would be the state of music and musicians in the days to come? Would he be pushed to repent for discontinuing his education? Pantulu cleared all his doubts. The status of music would only reach its acme by Murali. He will certainly rule the world of music as its uncrowned monarch.

Balamuralikrshna stopped going to the school and put an end to his academic studies. Pattabhiramayya engaged a teacher, privately, to teach Murali the subjects of English, Telugu, Sanskrit etc.

Once Balamurali broadcast from All India Radio, Madras. When he came out of the studios, an English lady, who was all along sitting in the foyer and listening to the programme, approached Pattabhiramayya and complimented him. The father and the son were dumbstruck, not being able to reply and about this Balamuralikrshna narrated later:

"We were unable to answer the lady. I felt much ashamed over this. When we went back to Vijayawada, I requested my private tutor to make me fully conversant in English. He told me, that English was not so easy to learn. It was not music, which I had imbibed from birth. He asked me to be diligent and with rapt attention and hard practice to study at least for one year. He was really an able teacher and that's why, my father engaged him for a monthly salary of fifteen rupees, a considerable amount in those days. He started to teach me conversational English. In about four months, I was able to speak many sentences myself". We cannot say that the proficiency Balamuralikrshna acquired in English was solely due to the teacher. If we hear his present day orations in English, which are in parallel to his sweet music, we cannot but rest, assured that this is also yet another gift of God.

Sooryanarayanamurthi (S.N. Murthi) belonged to Vijayawada and had close association with the Mangalamapalli family. His wife learnt music from Pattabhiramayya. Murthi was then serving All India Radio at Madras, as a Programme Executive (later he retired as the Deputy Director General). During one of his visits to Vijayawada, he went to Pattabhiramayya's house and heard Balamurali's music. He told Pattabhiramayya that because of his job at Madras, he enjoyed many opportunities to listen to the music of great artistes of Tamilnadu. Since the boy's music was really superb he should be exposed in a fitting manner, in Madras also. He promised to send a contract to Balamurali, as soon as he returned to Madras, for a radio broadcast. Auditions were not necessary then, as it is today. The engagements offered to any artiste would only be at the discretion of the director. The directors also were knowledgeable in music, in those days. Soon Balamurali got the contract.

Pattabhiramayya went to Madras with his son for the broadcast on 2.7.1941 and this was the first programme of Balamuralikrshna, in All India Radio. In the South, there was only the Madras station of AIR, at that time. Artistes from Tamilnadu, Andhra, and Mysore had their broadcasting assignments only at Madras. Among the musicians of Andhra Pradesh, Parupalli Ramakrshnayya Pantulu alone had the privilege of giving programmes through AIR, Madras. Therefore, getting a chance there was a great thing. Almost all the *vidwans* of the South listened to the above programme of Balamurali. They were surprised to know that a boy of about ten years, singing beyond one's imagination. Some organisers also, after listening to the radio broadcast, wrote to Balamurali, seeking dates.

The rising fame of Murali proportionately engaged his father Pattabhiramayya for he had to look after the household needs, replying to number of letters and so on. Balamurali, on the other hand, had no worry at all. He never paid any special attention to did any practice to keep his voice in shape. Singing was one among his childhood plays. Even today, he does not practise or do rehearsal before the concert and never prepares a list of items to be rendered. These would occur in his mind, only on the platform. Since opportunities to give programmes in the south was on the rise, he practised few Tamil songs. Some patriotic songs were also ready with him. Barring the programmes in the South and the radio broadcasts, the stock accompanists to Balamurali, then, were Sarade Subba Rao (violin) and Radhakrshna Raju (*mrudangam*).

Rajuguru, who later worked as a lecturer in *Mrudangam* in the Government College of Music, Vijayawada, once reminisced to us:

"To accompany Murali was a mind boggling affair in many ways. Trains were not many in those days and hence they would always be crowded. Whenever we had to travel, I, a sturdy person, would rush into the coach, as soon as the train stopped and reserve two seats for Pattabhiramayya and Murali. Then I would take in the instruments and other things, through the window. We always travelled only by Inter class. I am reminded of an incident.

Once myself and Sarade Subba Rao got into the coach with Murali. Pattabhiramayya was handing over the luggage through the window, himself standing on the platform. At that time, a fellow picked his pocket. The purse which contained our journey tickets and about eighty rupees of cash was lost. Pattabhiramayya started to run after the thief. Not knowing what to do, we got out of the train. He reached the far end of the platform and caught hold of him. But, in a second's time, that thief threw away the purse beneath the coach. Luckily, some passenger standing nearby fetched it and with his help, Pattabhiramayya handed over the thief to the police. When he returned triumphantly, we once again boarded the train, which was delayed by ten minutes. On another occasion, we were standing on the Madras Central Station. There was a heavy crowd in the booking counter. Pattabhiramayya gave eight *annas* to the booking clerk, sitting inside, and managed to get the tickets. A CID Inspector, who was watching this, came there and charge sheeted the clerk for taking bribe, making Pattabhiramayya a witness. The case went on for months and Pattabhiramayya had to make trips to Madras, for every hearing in the court. So much for the difficulty in those days, when we had to undertake a train travel. But all this would vanish, as soon as, we listened to the voice of Murali, in the concert. We felt scary during his *swaraprastaras*. He would go on doing them and none could anticipate what would come next. We never considered it below our prestige to accompany a very small boy. In age only he was young, but in music, he stood in high. We were, and even today are proud of him".

Many artistes of Tamilnadu enjoyed the pleasure of providing accompaniment to Balamurali. In a marriage concert on 25.9.1942, in the house of Devakottai Annamalai Chettiar, the violinist was Palakkadu C.R. Mani Iyer and the *mrudangist* was Karaikkudi Muthu Iyer. Mayuram Govindaraja Pillai, Kuttalam Sivavadivelu Pillai and Aalngudi Ramachandran accompanied Balamurali on the violin, *mrudangam* and *ghatam*, respectively, in the house of Lakshmanan Chettiar, at Nattarasankottai, on 3.6.1942. In Kandaramanickam, Balamurali gave a recital with K.C. Tyagarajan (violin), Umayalpuram Ganesa Iyer (*mrudangam*), Alangudi Ramachandran (*ghatam*), Karaikkudi Natesa Iyer *(dholak)* and Nettakudi Harihara Saram (*mukhasangu*). This is called a 'full-bench' concert. This type of concerts was more usual with Kancheepuram Naina Pillai and his disciple, Chittoor Subramania Pillai. Balamurali was only twelve then. Another 'full-bench' Programme he gave on 6.8.1943 at Paganeri, with K.C. Tyagarajan on the violin, Tirugokarnam Meenakshi-sundaram on the *mrudangam*, Panangudi Chellam Iyer on the *khanjira* and Avudyarkovil Harihara Bhagavatar on the *gettuvadya*.

The performance that won great fame to Balamurali was the one in the Tyagaraja festival at Tiruvaiyaru. It was only this programme that introduced him to a large circle of *vidwans* and *rasikas* in Tamilnadu.

Parupalli Ramakrshnayya Pantulu came to Madras with Pattabhiramayya and Balamurali on 25.12.1941. Under the auspices of Madras Andhra Maha Sabha, Balamurali gave a performance on 28.12.1941 and in the Jagannatha Bhakta Sabha, on the last day of the year. Pattabhiramayya was regular in writing letters to his sister in law, Subbamma, during his outstation camps. On such letter runs as:

29.12.41, Madras

"....Your card reached me. We are fine here and came to know of the matters, conveyed by you. Chi. Krshna is fine and healthy. Day before yesterday, we came from Venkataratnam's place to the house where Guruji is staying. Yesterday, the programme in Andhra Maha Sabha went off very well. On 31st, there is a concert in Jagannatha Bhakta Sabha. Everything goes on well. After completing all the engagements we shall return, for the festival. I shall bring a secondhand fiddle for Satyam, if available. No panicky situation here because of war...."

—M. Pattabhiramayya

"Dear Amma, Namaskara. I am fine. Yesterday's programme was well responded and a silver cup was presented to me. After finishing the programmes here, we will go to Tiruvaiyaru. Please take care of yourself. Hope Parvati and others are fine."

—M. Balamurlikrshna

'Satyam' mentioned in this letter is the renowned musician, Nookala Chinna Satyanarayana, then a disciple of Pattabhiramayya. After finishing Balamurali's radio programme on 2.1.1942, all the three went to Tiruvaiyaru, and reached the place in the early hours of 5.1.1942. With a devout desire to introduce his disciple, Balamuralikrshna, to all musical luminaries and *rasikas* of the south, who use to assemble in Tiruvaiyaru, Pantulu requested the festival organisers to give the time allotted to him, to his young ward. The rest of the incidence has already been narrated. Speaking about his *Guru's* broad heart, Balamurali gave us another anecdote.

"My *guru* and I had been to a *sabha* at Madras, to listen to some prominent musician's concert. Due to indisposition, that vocalist didn't turn up and the *sabha* secretary was requesting the violin *vidwan* to play a solo. How nice it would be, I thought, if someone asks my *guru*, to sing on that day. Exactly at that time, my *guru* got up from his seat and went inside the office room. Although his request to provide me the opportunity to sing there, bore no fruit, I felt hundred times dwarfed before his generosity. All through his lifetime, he spared no efforts to uplift his disciples. Never did he want to sing himself and jealousy and envy are the two words, unknown to him"

The Second World War was going on. Though India did not take part directly, its soldiers were in the British army and throughout the country, there was panic among the people as to when the country would be bombed. Under such circumstances, Balamuralikrshna had to travel far and wide, fulfilling his concert commitments. In spite of the surrounding fear, people thronged to his performances, with a desire not to miss the golden opportunity. He had engagements not only in Andhra and Tamilnadu, but also in places like Orissa, Kashmir and Mysore. When Pattabhiramayya was away with his son, Parupalli would himself accept concerts for Balamurali and communicate it. An extract from one of his letters:

"Srirastu Bezawada, 23.3.1943

Blessings to Chi. Mangalampalli Pattabhiramayya. I have accepted the following programmes for our Chi. Balamurali.

25.3.43 - Marriage in the house of Mullapudi Zamindar, Sri Timmaraju. Received ten rupees as advance against the remuneration of rupees one hundred and sixty, inclusive of Sarade Subba Rao, Radhakrshna Raju and the expenses. So, proceed to Tanuku on that date.

Chi. Murali has already been engaged on 27th Ganapavaram and so I have accepted a concert for him on 29.3.1943 at Tenali, in the marriage function held in a Sowcar's house. Rupees one hundred and fifty would be paid there inclusive of Sarade and Raju. Rupees twenty five given as advance is with me. Therefore, you have to come here as soon as the Ganapavaram programme is over....".

Even at such a young age, Balamurali was giving chain of performances. Sometimes he had to give more than two hundred concerts in a year. The table given below showing his engagements during the year 1943, would help to understand how much Balamurali was sought after. Concerts in *sabhas*, festivals and radio programmes have not been included in this table.

4.1.1943	- Ongole	17.5.1943	- Nidadavolu
9.2.1943	- Guntoor	18.5.1943	- Alamooru
12.2.1943	- Akhiripalle	21.5.1943	- Tanuku
14.2.1943	- Bheemadolu	28.5.1943	- Vizianagaram
20.2.1943	- Akiveedu	31.5.1943	- Rajamundry
25.2.1943	- Hyderabad	6.6.1943	- Nidadavolu
28.2.1943	- Undi	11.6.1943	- Peravali
5.3.1943	- Achanta	13.6.1943	- Bapatla
21.3.1943	- Kadali	17.6.1943	- Kodilanka
25.3.1943	- Tanuku	26.6.1943	- Narasannapeta
27.3.1943	- Ganapavaram	24.7.1943	- Amalapuram
29.3.1943	- Tenali	8.10.1943	- Narasapur
12.4.1943	- Pedda Pulleru	7.11.1943	- Guntur
15.4.1943	- Tadepalligudem	13.11.1943	- Rajamundry
16.4.1943	- Palacole	15.11.1943	- Guntur
28.4.1943	- Ankapalle	15.12.1943	- Ongole
30.4.1943	- Puthem	20.12.1943	- Secunderabad
11.5.1943	- Eluru	24.12.1943	- Secunderabad

Such hectic and continuous engagements were not only in his younger days, but continued until he, few years back, retired from professional singing. If anybody wanted his programmes, they had to fix him up, at least four months in advance.

"Andhra Saraswata Parishad" is a cultural organisation in Andhra Pradesh and was steered by great scholars of different categories. 'Sahiteevallabha' Raja Venkatadri Appa Rao, *Zamindar* of Vuyyur was its president and the members were: 'Sahitya Samrat' Raja Vikrama Varma, Dr. Kattamanchi Ramalinga Reddi, Dr. Chilukoori Narayana Rao, 'Darsanacharya' Koochimanchi Gopalakrshnayya, Varnasi Venkatasubrahmany Sastri, 'Kala Prapoorna' Janamanchi Seshadri Sarma, Dr. Vetoori Prabhakara Sastri 'Gayaka Sarvabhouma' Parupalli Ramakrshnayya Pantulu, 'Vainika Sikhamani' Muluku Sivananda Sastri, 'Sangeeta Sahitya' Satyavolu Radhamadhava Kavi, 'Vidya Vachaspati' Pulya Umamahcsware Sastri and 'Sahitya Visarada' Kona Venkataraya Sarma. In one of its meeting, the parishad resolved to take the pride of first felicitating Balamurlikrshna, ahead of others, with a title.... It arranged a grand function on 15.1.1943 at Nuzvid and paid its tributes to Balamuralikrshna and awarded the title "Ganga Sudhakara". This was the first instance in the annals of music, a thirteen year old boy was honoured with a fitting title. Today, we find it common, many musicians request the impresarios to arrange a felicitation and to confer a title with a golden shawl, on an understanding that all the expenses would be borne by the concerned musician. But this was not the case with Balamuralikrshna, then and now. He had secured innumerable awards and titles; shawls and medals. He never aspired for one nor they came to him, sponsored by any 'Sugar daddy'.

Wealth competed with his *Vidwat*, even before he completed the age of fifteen. 'Poverty' was a word, now not known to Pattabhiramayya. He had since stopped cycling to the homes of his students and had to be choosy in having students, that too, only in his house. In fact, he found it difficult to spare time to sit and teach even such select students. At times, he had to be out of station, even continually for a fortnight. While in headquarters, he was kept engaged in purchasing household provisions and replying to letters that had piled up. Now he could demand a higher fee for Balamurali's programmes, even from All India Radio. It is with this idea, that he declined a contract sent by S.N. Murthi for a broadcast on 4.4.1943, the Telugu New Year's Day. Some friends suggested to him that it would not be fair to refuse a programme on a New Year's Day for sentimental reasons. Pattabhiramayya did not heed it. But this, in no way, severed the cordial relationship of Balamurali with AIR. He honoured all the contracts he received for broadcasting on 1.7.1943, 11.11.1943 and 30.12.1943.

Maharaja Swati Tirunal, Pandit Jawaharlal Nehru and such others were mentioned as 'Garbha Sreeman' (born with silver spoon in the mouth). Likewise, it would not be an exaggeration, if we mention Balamuralikrshna as 'Garbha Vidyavan' (born with all arts). He became not only an outstanding vocalist, but showed remarkable talent in handling the violin, the *mrudangam* and so on.

In his childhood, he used to pick up two small twigs out of the broomstick and keeping one vertically as if a violin drew with the other, horizontally, supposing it as the bow. Subbamma would shout, "What are you doing? If the whole broomstick is destroyed like this, how could I sweep the house?" Immediately, Murali would throw that away and start to drum the brass vessels, kept in the kitchen. Again Subbamma would admonish him, "This is very good. Only recently, your father purchased these few vessels. What will happen to them, if you beat like this? Do one thing. From tomorrow, tap on my head". Unable to tolerate this regular mischief, she advised Pattabhiramayya to procure a small violin and a *mrudangam* for the boy, if at all he wanted to safeguard the household goods. After some time, Pattabhiramayya purchased these two and Balamurali's practice commenced on both. The father, later, described: "Surprisingly, he showed extraordinary mastery on the violin too. Exposure would come if only he accompanies someone. 'Solos' were not in vogue, in those days. One day, I asked him, whether he would play on the violin in a public concert. He had no objection but with one condition that he would first accompany only Pantulugaru. But, who would dare to ask Guruji to have Murali as his violin accompanist? First of all, Pantulugaru must be satisfied with the boy's skill. We were worried but not for long. Time came soon, Guruji himself asked Murali to accompany him".

The news that Balamurali showed prowess on the violin reached Paruapilli's ears. One day, during the class hours, he asked Murali casually about it. When he got an affirmative reply, he brought his own instrument, gave it to him and asked to play for a while. Murali's playing made him dumbfounded. He arranged Murali's violin accompaniment for his own vocal recital, in the Aradhana Festival of Susarla Dakshinamurthi Sastri. The next such performance was on a day during the Dasara festival in the Durga Malleeswara temple. The guru's vocal to the violin accompaniment continued for years. Benefit performances in aid of Sri Gopalakrshna Bhakta Sodari Mandali, were held under the aegis of Andhra Gana Maha Sabha of Secunderabad. Balamuralikrshna gave a vocal recital on 5.1.1945 and on the next day, he accompanied Parupalli on the violin, many *sabhas* arranged 'dual' concerts. One such programme was held in Baramapuram. His vocal concert was on 15.4.1954 and, next day, he bowed the violin in the vocal recital by Palakkadu K.V. Narayanaswami with Palakkadu Mani Iyer on the *mrudangam.* On some earlier occasions too, he had accompanied some artistes of Tamilnadu.

Next to his *guru,* Balamuralikrshna provided violin accompaniment to G.N. Balasubramaniam in the year 1943. G.N. Balasubramaniam was overwhelmed with joy, when he listened to Murali's violin playing in that concert, held in Rajamundry. He always preferred only Balamurali's violin accompaniment. Whenever he visited Andhra Pradesh and if anyone else had not been already arranged by the organiser. G.N. Balasubramaniam used to say, "The style of both of us are almost the same and we are one, so to say".

Ariyakkudi Ramanuja Iyengar, the doyen of Carnatic music, was slated to give a vocal performance at Machilipatnam, in the house of the Gandrekula *zamindar*, in 1944. It was in connection with a marriage celebration. Though the responsibility of arranging the accompanists was left to Iyengar, he arrived without a violinist. In enquiry, he said that the violinist could not come due to some urgent and personal work in his native village. He was of the idea that someone locally could be easily arranged. The agents of the *zamindar* hurried to many players of that town but non was ready to accept. Varanasi Bráhmayya, Subbayya and many other excused themselves saying that they were not that much competent to accompany the leonine Iyengar. The *zamindar* called one Acharya, who was looking after the hospitality of the visiting artistes and asked him the position. At that time, someone casually suggested the name of Balamuralikrshna. Acharya was immediately packed up in a car and sent to Vijayawada to bring Balamurali.

It was eleven O'clock, when Acharya entered "Sooryakanta Bhavanam" and he explained the situation, in detail and prayed to Pattabhiramayya to come with his son and help. The father who already knew well Acharya, pronounced his inability. "Look Acharya! though I have no objection, it is not possible today, because, Murali is running a high temperature. For the past three days he is indisposed. Come in and see for yourself". Murali was lying on a cot, just after taking a cup of gruel. When Acharya enquired about his condition, Murali replied that he felt better. Acharya turned towards Pattabhiramayya and resumed his request, "I have no other go. He need not play at all; it is enough if he occupies the place with the violin. Please". Subbamma intervened and asked Acharya to stop talking nonsense, even after himself witnessing the condition of the already weak boy. But Acharya persistently pestered that it was not for saving the prestige of the *zamindar* but only that of Andhra Pradesh. These words had an impact on the mind of Murali. Was it not his duty to save the prestige of his own Andhradesa? He slowly got up and said, "Father! he requests you so much. I can manage. Shall we go?" None could say a second word and Acharya arrived in Machilipatnam with Balamuralikrshna and his father, at four, that evening.

Coming to know that a boy of fourteen years was going to accompany him, Ramanuja Iyengar was surprised. He had already heard about Balamuralikrshna, from persons of his own place, Chettinadu. He also knew that the boy had swayed the entire assemblage in Tiruvaiyaru, by his superb music, at the age of ten or so. In fact, his own concert time was given to the boy for extending the programme on that day. But could it mean that he was equally adept in handling the violin? Anyway he had to manage the show. With this thought, Iyengar sent his disciple to the place, where Balamuralikrshna was staying, with the message that the boy need not worry and could play without any fear. To adjust him, Iyengar would alleviate his usual standard. Balamurali's respect and regard for Iyengar only enhanced on hearing these words. He sent back a reply, verbally, that the great man need not mind a small boy, sitting beside him. Lots of people from various other towns also had assembled there, only to enjoy the maestro's music. In spite of his own indisposition, he had accepted the invitation only to listen to the unsurpassable music of Iyengar. Therefore, Iyengar need not lessen his standard, on any account. It would only be disappointing the *rasikas*. Moreover no room should be given for anyone to think that Iyengar was a stuffy person. He sent the messenger back, asking him to pass on his salutations.

The eagerly awaited concert began with the *varna* in the *raga kalyani*, set to *ata tala*. The audience was keenly watching how Murali was going to manage. In the first two items, Ramanuja Iyengar gave no chance to Balamurali to play either *raga alapana* or *swara-prastara*. As time passed on, he realised that the boy was not a mediocre artiste, as he had presumed earlier.

On the contrary, he seemed to be a formidable and seasoned artiste. This realisation induced him to provide later copious opportunities to Balamurali. The *zamindar* and Acharya wondered how the boy, lying with fever even an hour ago, could play in such a competent a manner. In the *Raga-tana-pallavi* that followed, Murali exhibited his profound mastery. Ramanuja Iyengar blessed him profusely and exclaimed, "You are very intelligent! May Lord Raghava bless you with a long life".

Few days after the aforesaid incident, Chittor Subramania Pillai had been to Vijayawada and Balamurali accompanied him on the violin. Pillai was a colossus in doing *swaraprastara* in a complex manner. At the close of the concert, he patted on the back of Balamurali and said, "No one can cheat you in *swaraprastara*. I am surprised to see that you are 'at home' in any type of complicated manipulations of the *swaraprastara*."

Suribabau was a popular stage and cine actor in Andhra. He and his actress-wife, Rajeswari, were living in Satyanarayanapuram, opposite to Balmurali's house. One night he came to "Sooryakanta Bhavanam" and complimented Murali. Two days earlier when he happened to hear Balamurli's violin-playing, he felt that it was only some gandharva playing, having come down to earth. Suribabau praised Murali in high terms and presented a violin to the boy, which he had brought with him. The instrument was lying in his lumber room for many years. Instead of keeping it further dust-soiled and without any use, he thought it would be of some use to Murali. The latter received the present with respect. On opening the box and examining it, Balamurali's face bloomed. He said, "You, a great personality, have blessed me by presenting this. In fact, I have been desiring, for quite some time, to play on a viola, instead of a violin, which would be something unusual. Today it has come as God-sent, through you. This is a viola, not a violin. It will definitely be of great use to me for improvement of my playing". Next day, Pattabhiramayya took the viola to Lanka Venkateswarlu, who was an expert also in repairing musical instruments. In a week's time, the instrument came back, afresh with a new bow and box. From then on, Balamuralikrshna began to play only on the viola, in the place of a violin. The connoisseurs of music, even today, enjoy his viola music in public concerts, as well as over the radio.

Viola — the 'alto' of the string quartette called 'Violino Ordinario' was devised around 1600 and earned the status as the 'Chief of the Violins' though it appears just like a violin, it is slightly bigger in size. Only guts or thickly coiled strings are used for the viola, so that the sound produced is richer than on a violin. The viola cannot be tuned to the pitch more than E and the placement of *swaras* on the finger-board will also be distant from each other, unlike the violin. For the same reason, it is not that much easy to play it, in comparison to the violin. The credit of playing Carnatic music, for this first time, on the violin goes to Tanjavur Vadivelu (one among the Tanjavur Quartctte). Some others say that it was only Balaswami Dikshitar, younger brother of Muthuswami Dikshitar (of the Musical Trinity). But there could never be a second opinion on mentioning that Balamuralikrshna is the first to use viola in Carnatic music concerts.

In the same manner, Murali acquired expertise in handling the *mrudangam* also. By keenly observing the fingering teachinque employed by Radhakrshna Raju, he would try his hand on the samll instrument, procured by his father. Pattabhiramayya and Radhakrshna Raju while they were entering the farmer's house, on an evening, were astonished to hear a solo by Murali on the percussion. They wanted to bring it to light. Everybody knew that Balamurali would be very specific that he would first accompany only his *guru*. Ramakrshnayya Pantulu had a programme in the Durgapuram Dasara Festival. Balamurali ascended on the stage, prostrated before his *guru*, who had already occupied the central seat and sat on his right side. It took no time for Pantulu to understand that the boy was going to play the *mrudangam*. Raju brought and placed the *mrudangam* in front of Murali. Pantulu had been originally informed that Radhakrshna Raju would be the *mrudangist.* He inquisitively glanced at Raju. Getting up from his seat, Raju, submitted, "We have heard him many a time playing the *mrudangam* and he is very good at it. This is his debut programme as a *mrudangist.* You know his principle that he would display the art first only with you and your blessing. It is I who wanted him to take my place. Please excuse me for having not informed you about this, in advance. But I am confident that he would be able to please you". Pantulu smilingly said, "When you made him sit here, then itself I understood that he would play very well and I have no doubt at all. All is the grace of Goddess Durga". It is needless to describe how marvellously Balamurali would have played on the *mrudangam.* Music, in its different manifestation, had been planted in him by God, even before he stepped down on the earth. How else this phenomenon could be explained?

"Akila Andhra Patrika", a weekly published from Srikakulam, contained a review on Balamurali's music, in its issue dated 4.10.1943. An excerpt:

"Balamuralikrshna - a multifaceted artiste. Besides being an exemplary vocalist, he is adept in playing on the violin also. Ariyakudi Ramanuja Iyenger, G.N. Balasubramaniyam, Parupalli Ramakrshnayya Pantulu and such other musical giants may be mentioned as few among many, whom Balamurali has accompanied on the violin. Next, he displays extreme mastery over the *mrudangam* also, though it is only a hobby for him. I listened to a programme by Voleti Venkateswarlu, a *vidwan* on the staff of All India Radio, Vijayawada, with Annavarupa Ramaswami on the violin and Balamurali on the *mrudangam.* I was immensely pleased to hear Balamurali's virtuosity on that instrument. It will not be an exaggeration, if we call him a 'savyaschi' (translated by the author) 'Savyaschi' means ambidexter. The above review was written by Danappa Bhagavatar.

In the course of time, opportunities came to both the *guru* and the disciple, to play on many occasions.

Pantulu would usually sit in front and enjoy Murali's singing and would be delighted to note all others around him were equally appreciative. Sometimes, he would suggest to the organisers to arrange Balamurali's violin or *mrudangam*, for his own recitals.

During my *gurukulavasa* days at Vijayawada, I have had the opportunity of listening to my guruji's *mrudangam* playing, on so many occasions. In the evenings he would ask M.V. Ramanamurthi (a good vocalist, now no more) to sing and he would play on the *mrudangam*. Tanjavur Upendran (a front-ranking *mrudanga vidwan*, an intimate friend and admirer of Balamuralikrshna; he passed away few years before) used to come to and stay at Vijayawada for some days. On such occasions, when either my *guruji* or Upendran had no concert engagements, the evening soirees would have Upendran's *mrudangam* and my *guruji's khanjira*. Sometimes, while resting in the afternoons, *guruji* would ask us (his disciples) to sing with him sitting with the *khanjira*. Thousands of *rasikas* enjoyed his playing on the *khanjira*, in the violin solo recital by Lalgudi G. Jayaraman, during the Aradhana festival of 1977, in Tiruvaiyaru.

Once I asked my *guru*, "You have already exhibited your profound skill on the violin, viola, *mrudangam* and *khanjira*, not to speak about your insuperable vocal music. What else do you know to play?" "Many" was his reply and I waited for an explanation. He continued: "I can play Veena, Harmonium, Gottuvadayam, flute and so on. But I don't touch the flute, for my father had taken a promise from me. His worry was that I will become emaciated physically, since one has to blow air on the flute. Of course, air is coming out, even while singing; but that is different from blowing into a wind instrument. I can very well play on the veena, the instrument most cherished by my mother. I have taught one or two students in veena playing. But the fingering technique, at times, handicaps my playing on the viola. So I generally don't play that. Bring that *tambura*". He took the *tambura* from me, keeping it horizontally and using a fountain pen as a wedge, he began to play the *raga*, Sahana followed by Sindhubhairavi. "This is nothing but Gottuvadyam", he said. I was stupefied.

Novelty is a thing always in the blood of my *guruji*, Balamuralikrshna. Opening new vistas in the art of music was his innate love. Some years back, he did a novel thing, for the first time in history, thanks to the advanced technology in electronics. He cut a gramophone disc, in which he has sung 'Adamodigalada', a Tyagaraja *kriti* in the *raga charukesi*, with *raga alapana*, niraval and *swaraprastara*. Viola and *mrudangam* support have also been provided by himself, including a percussive solo. 'Time sense' is an important requisite to do such a marvel and he is proficient in that. Musicians know the difficulty in executing the 'Kuraippu' (*swaras* in gradually reduced *tala* cycles) during the *swaraprastara*. Unless one has a precise 'time sense', it would be not possible to do so, that too, when the same individual has to do a tridimensional job — vocal, viola and *mrudangam* playing — everything in perfectly precise manner. It cannot be described by means of words. Only when one listens to this gramophone disc, the immaculate 'time sense' of Balamuralikrshna can be perceived. This record is a monumental achievement. I jocularly asked my *guruji*, "Why didn't you include the *khanjira*?", to which he smiled and said, "It's alright... let me do that also later". How befitting it is to call him a "*Garbha Vidyavani*"

Music, composing *sahitya*, dance, painting, sculpture and many others constitute 'Fine Arts'. Balamurlikrshna's accomplishments, include drawing and painting. Some of his works, done at an early age, are still preserved. They introduce Balamurali to us, as a fine artist. Had he not devoted his heart and time to music, he would have come up as a 'Number One' painter.

"Somehow, he inculcated a desire to paint in his younger days. Whenever he found a piece of paper and a pencil he would draw some figures. Twenty days in a month, at least, we had to travel, for music concerts. When in Vijayawada, his music lessons and classes with the private instructor, consumed most of his time. Time constraints deprived Murali from playing whole-hearted attention to painting and in due course, his interest subsided" — these are the words of Pattabhiramayya.

Composing *sahitya* (musical lyric) requires much knowledge. One should be well-versed in '*Sahitya Lakshana*' and usages of proper words. Whenever the Sanskrit teacher started to explain the poetic *genius* of Kalidasa, Murali would mentally indulge in the beauties of the poems and imbibed an urge that he should also compose, at least, in the near future. This avidity increased, day by day. In one of his concerts, he met the great poet, Kasi Krshnacharyulu and expressed his desire to him. Krshnacharyulu had much affection towards Murali and unless otherwise engaged, he never missed attending the boy's concerts, anywhere in the town. When Murali now asked for his guidance, the poet was reminded of Sri Tyagaraja. He promised to send some books that would help Murali in composing and blessed him, "May God bless you to blossom as an insurmountable *vaggeyakara*". Nobody at that time ever dreamt that Krshnacharyulu's words would come true. Today Balamuralikrshna tops the list of contemporary *vaggeyakaras*. Krshnacharyulu sent some books the next day and Balamurali memorised every word in them. At the outset, he composed one or two lines, to be used as '*pallavis*'. '*Pallavi*' is short *sahitya*, unlike the *kriti*, to be used as a 'piece de resistance' in the Carnatic music. Normally, it would be preceded by a lengthy essaying of the *raga* and its medium tempo phrasings called *tana*. To do the *Niraval* (expansion of the lyrical letters) and *swaraprastara* is considered as a test to the calibre of an artists. The following are some of Balamurali's early stage *Pallavi* compositions:

1. Amba Kalyani Sambhu Rani — Kalyani — Tisra Jhampa.
2. Mamava Sankara Umadhava — Begada — Adi.
3. Sree Raghuvara mamava srutajanapalaka — Kambhoji — Sankeerna Jhampa.
4. Mohanangi Kalyani Pahimam — Anandabhairavi —

Ragamalika consisting of the ragas, Mohana, Kalyani and Ananadabhairavi — Adi.

5. Anandamrutavrshini Jananee Pahimam — Apara Karunakari Sacchidanandabhairavi — Ragamalika, consisting of the ragas, Amrutavarshini and Anandabhairavi — Tisra Jhampa (Sankeerna Gati).
6. Paramapavani Pahimam Varade Haimavati Lalite — Hemavati — Lalita tala.

In this above *sahitya*, the names of the *raga* and *tala*, *Hemavati* and *Lalita*, respectively, have been incorporated. *Pallavi* wizards were doing, *Rettai Pallavis*, some decades ago. *Rettai* means 'double' or 'pair' and *Rattai Pallavis* would be in two *talas*; the first part - *Poorvanga* - in one *tala* and the latter part - *Uttaranga* - another. Few *Pallavis* given in the above list are not only *Rettai Raga Pallavis*, but sometimes in more than two *ragas*. Balamurali is the first musician to do such *pallavis*. Besides these, Balamuralikrshna had composed many *pallavi sahityas*, spontaneously, to suit the occasion. The *pallavi "Jayamimma! Jaya hayana ma sada maku"* may be a good specimen. This is in the *raga*, Jayasree (a derivative of Keeravani Mela) and the *tala* is, incidentally, 'Digjaya' (having eleven *aksharas*). The occasion was the birth of the New Year, *Jaya*. Similarly, Balamuralikrshna composed and sang a *pallavi* (in a *Raga - Tana - Pallavi* recital) broadcast by the Madras station of All India Radio, in 1970. The *Pallavi*, *"Sarigamapadhani Padeda - sacchinanada dayini"* took its birth only inside the studios, about ten minutes before the broadcast. It is in the *raga*, Shanmukhapriya set to Tisra Jhampa *tala* in Khanda *gati*. Generally, Balamurali never repeated any *pallavi*, for a second time, unless he was requested to do so. He is capable of composing any number of *pallavis* or *kritis*, in a moment's time, studded with some novelty in it. That is yet another uniqueness of Balamuralikrshna.

I want to mention here about one of his 'brain-teasing' *pallavis*. That concert in the music Academy, Madras, raised the eyebrows of many. He rendered a *pallavi*, "*nagaswaravalihite — parama hamsadhwani virajite*", in two *ragas*, namely *Nagaswaravali* and *Hamsadhwani*. But the technique he adopted to sing these two *ragas* was unprecedented. *Nagaswaravali* has 's g m p d s — s d p m g s' as its *arohana* and *avarohana*, while Hamsadhwani has 's r g p n s — s n p g r s', both pentatonic. If the *madhyama* of *Nagaswaravali* is taken as *shadja*, by the method of Modal shift of Tonic, the result would be *Hamsadhwani*. Balamuralikrshna employed this and rendered it. The *Poorvanga* (first section) — Nagaswaravalihite — was in *Nagaswaravli raga*, while the *Uttaranga* (latter section) — *Parama Hamsadhwani* virajite — was also rendered in the same *Nagaswaravali raga*, but taking its *madhyama* as *shadja*, thereby sounding it as *hamsadhwani*. The *tala* was Tisra Jhampa in *khanda gati*. This rare feat, he executed in three speeds of tempo, effortlessly. To pass comments, even appreciatively, on witnessing one's acrobatics on trapeze would be easy for anyone, but the difficulty and risk involved are know only to the acrobat. Music is abstract and cannot be explained with mere words. Victor Hugo wrote, "Music expresses that which cannot be said and on which, it is impossible to be silent". Many musicians in the audience, that day, were awe-struck. In the beginning, it was not easy for them to perceive what was being done on the stage. It took time for them to recover from the stupor. Soon after the concert, many went on the dais and appreciated Balamuralikrshna's tantalising *pallavi* and the novel manner of execution that could never be imagined by anyone else. Some of his close friends asked him, why he ventured to demonstrate such an intricacy. *Guruji* smilingly said, "If not in the Music Academy, where else? I know many of the musicians and *rasikas*, sitting in the auditorium, could not enjoy the intricacy". During his formative years, some people doubted whether words in the form of an address to God, could be construed as *a sahitya*, although such a doubt has no base or necessity. 'Kavi Samrat' Viswanatham, a great Telugu literature, wrote in this connection:

"It cannot be denied that sweet sound is possessed by such *Sambodhana padas*; the arrangement of the words and its order should be given importance, without any detriment to the prosody. Don't we have plenty of poets, connected with our Telugu literature, who have simply used sweet words?"

The lyric, particularly for *Pallavi* is normally not a lengthy one, but should be in conformity with the rules laid down by the musical decalogue. Every letter should rest at its own place, during the *Niraval*. The lyric should, on no account, give room for any deviation or adjustment. The *sahityas* of Balamuralikrshna stick to all these rules. His desire to compose *kritis*, was fuelled by a great saint.

His holiness Vimalananda Bharati was the Pontiff of Kutralam Peetham. He was the spiritual *guru* of Parupalli Ramakrshnayya Pantulu and an ardent lover of music. Right form the day of Balamuralikrshna's debut, he became an aficionado of the prodigy. It was only on his suggestion, Harinagabhushanam arranged Murali's concert at Machilipatnam. In 1944, he came to Vijayawada, after touring many places, and was camping there. One afternoon, he sent one of his servants to fetch Murali. Swamiji asked Balamurali, who arrived without knowing why he was called, "Murali! what were you doing? Playing cards?" Actually, Balamurali was playing the game with some of his friends, when the messenger came. But it would be disrespectful to say so before Swamiji and so he replied, "I was studying some lessons in English". A dialogue ensued between them:

Swamiji: So, you were not practising music?

Murali: Only this morning, I had been to *guruji's* house.

Swamiji: Is it? For the past few days, I am camping here — just opposite to your house. Not even a single day, your music reached my ears. Anyway, answer me. All of you, sing the *keertanas* of Tyagaraja and adore him as *Sadguru*. Was there music before him?

Murali: Certainly! Nadabraham is all pervading and music has neither a beginning nor an end.

Swamiji: Before him, was there any music concert?

Murali: I don't know. May be not, as it is today. I have heard that music programmes were held in royal courts. It seems music was not a profession, then.

Swamiji: If so, what would they have sung? That is before Tyagaraja?

Murali: Probably the compositions of Annamacharya, Purandaradasa and suchlike.

Swamiji: But why should everyone discard those after the advent of Tyagaraja? Only his compositions come to prominence today.

Murali: I do not know about the history of music. There are many reasons to revere Tyagaraja as great *vaggeyakara*. The lucid style in his *kritis*, a flow of lilting music, soaked in *bhakti*, more fitting to the meaning of the *sahitya* — all these may be mentioned. He has composed them, himself enjoying and tasting the *bhava*. That's why his *kritis* arc immortal.

Swamiji: You are absolutely right. In fact, I wanted to elicit these details from your mouth. Tyagaraja earned a special place, because he created something new; he innovated an individual style for himself. From this, we are made sure that an immortal name in history could be got only by those, who exhibit an individuality. This is applicable to you too. Since you started to sing at the age of ten, all praise you as the incarnation of Sarasvati. We are not sure, how long this will last. Day by day you are growing up as a man. Now they say, your music is wonder, but the same tongues may later say, "No wonder, an experienced person singing like this". I have not an iota of doubt in your bright and prosperous future and you will surely be regarded as the greatest musician of the times. But it is upto you to adopt something unique, with which your name will become immortal.

Murali: Swamiji! What should I do?

Swamiji: Let time come. God Himself will show you the way.

The conversation ended and Murali returned home, blessed by the saint. That night he was reclining on the cot, reflecting on Swamiji's words and was looking at the sky, through the window. After a shortwhile, the light hanging from the ceiling started to move here and there rapidly, as if caught in a storm. Some sound came from the switchboard, he got up and went to put off the light. As soon as he placed his hand on the switch, he got a shock and fell down. For about five minutes he was lying on the floor, without knowing what was happening. When he regained senses, he saw a big monkey sitting in front of him and he could neither move nor shout. The monkey paced towards him and dabbed with its hands on his head. He closed his eyes tightly, out of fear and when he opened them within a moment, the visitor was not to be seen anywhere. An idea flashed in his mind. For the past one month, he was contemplating about the dearth of *keertanas* in the seventy two *melaragas*, particularly in Sanskrit and Telugu. Now, it was a Divine command to him that he should start composing them. Yes! Lord Maruti had come to bless him. Right from his early days, he considered Anjaneya as his *ishta devata* and used to begin any writing only with obeisance to the monkey — God.

Without wasting even a minute, Balamurali took a sheet of paper and started to scribble a song, composed by him at that time. As was his wont, this first composition is "Guruni Smarimpumu" in the *raga, hamasavinodini,* in honour of his *guru*, Parupalli Ramakrshnayya Pantulu. Then came the *kritis* in the seventy two *melaragas*, one after the other. Lord Ganesa is praised in the first piece, in Kanakangi, *Sreesaputraya namostute.* Ratnangi, the second *melaraga* has *Sree Gurum Chintayami* on Sri Tyagaraja. Upto the fifth *melaraga*, Manavati, Balamuralikrshna composed *kritis*, in the consecutive order. The rest he did at random, not serially.

In the South Indian musical system, the early treatises on music mention the parent *ragas* (also called janaka *ragas* or mela *ragas)* under the name, Raganga *ragas*. Venkatamakhin (17th century) was the first to evolve the seventy two *melakarta* scheme based on twenty two *srutis*, logically. The basic seven *swaras* were given sixteen *swarasthanas*, with names for each. This ingenious scheme gives rise to numberless *raga* scales (janya *ragas* or derivative *ragas*) and is still in operation. We find many Tyagaraja *kritis* in some of these *melaragas*, but it was only Muthuswami Dikshitar, who composed in all the seventy two.

The first composition in the seventy two *melaragas*, as a *ragamalika*, is by Tanjavur 'Lavani' Venkata Rao (1817/7.5.1900). It is in praise of Sakharam Saheb, son-in-law of Sivaji, the last Maratha ruler of Tanjavur and is in Marathi. It is known as 'Bahattara Melaragamalika'. Venkata Rao was a disciple of Manambucchavadi Venkatasubbayya (Guru of Susarla Dakashinamurthi Sastri). Maha Vaidyanatha Iyer also had studied under the same Venkatasubbayya and was a good friend of Venkata Rao. The 'Bhattara Melaragamalika' of Venkata Rao inspired him to do one in praise of Lord Pranatarthihara, the presiding deity of Tiruviyaru. This *ragamalika* is in Sanskrit. After him, it was Koteeswara Iyer (1870/ 20.10.1938), who composed *kritis* in these *mela ragas*. These seventy two compositions in Tamil are entitled 'Kanda Ganamudam'. Balamuralikrshna is the next Vaggeyakara to compose *kritis* in all the seventy two *mela ragas*. Out of them, thirteen are in Telugu and the rest in Sanskrit. A very high standard of music is woven in all these, throughout and the composer's main aim was to project the *raga-swaroopa*. The name of the concerned *raga* has also been incorporated in many *kritis*. Literary beauties like alliteration are not scanty. For instance, the composition in the nineteenth *melaraga*, Jhankaradhwani, "Jashaketana" contains the letter *ja* at the beginning of every line. Chittaswaras have been appended in some, while the 'Swarakshara' usage is found in many others. Scholars are of the opinion that mastering these *kritis* of Balamuralikrshna properly, would considerably help one to acquire sound knowledge in elaboration of the *ragas* and to do *swaraprastara*, even in the *vivadi melaragas* (parent scales with some dissonant notes). While talking about these *melaraga kritis*, Balamurali explained: "Take the *raga* Charukesi, for example. The *swaras* are of Sankarabharanam in the lower tetrachord and of Todi in the upper tetrachord. But if one sings as such, it cannot be Charukesi. The difference in the use of *gamakas* in, say, two *ragas* with the same Rshabha and Gandhara, would explicitly bring out the *raga swaroopa*. Though there have been discussions going about this, no specific effort has been made. So, I thought about the need for clearly showing the real *swaroopa* of *ragas*, like this. The *swaroopa* could be expressed only with the help of a composition. Without a composition any *raga* would only remain a name in the books. So I composed these seventy two and other *janya raga kritis*. I tried in them to build in the *swara* combination which are the essence of these *ragas*, so that the *raga* and its *swaroopa* are at once apparent". It is true what Benjamin Disrelli wrote: "Man is made to create, from the poet to the potter".

The news about Balamuralikrshna's *melaraga kritis*, first reached the ears of Parupalli Ramakrshnayya Pantulu and through him to Bethapudi Sarabhayya. Sarabhayya was the one who presented Murali with a golden laced velvet apparel, after his maiden performance. He would always present something to the young singer, whenever he attended his performances. Now, on knowing about the new seventy two compositions of Murali, he felt very happy and volunteered to publish them. He asked Balamuralikrshna to sing one or two out of them, in the forthcoming programme in Durgapuram. The pleasure of the connoisseurs knew no bounds, when Balamurali sang "Sri Dakshinamurthim", in the *raga*, Keeravani, composed in honour of Susarla Dakshinamurthi Sastri, followed by the Naganandini Kriti, "Dakshayani".

Murali was sleeping, after having presented an enticing concert, the previous night, in Durgapuram. Subbamma came and woke him up with the words, "Ayyappa Sastri is waiting for more than half an hour, to see you, Get up and come". Balamurali came to the hall, where his father was conversing with Ayyappa Sastri. Pattabhiramayya asked him to quickly finish his bath and go with Sastri. Getting ready, Balamurali followed Ayyappa Sastri, without a word, like Rama, who followed Viswamitra, at the behest of Dasaratha.

Bhamidipati Ayyappa Sastri was a profound scholar in Sanskrit and Telugu. He was a close friend of Sarabhayya and moreover a *Durgadevi Upasaka*. Sastri entered his house and ushered in Murali inside his *pooja* room. He said: "You may wonder why I brought you here. Yesterday, I heard you sing your new compositions. Really they are very good. No one could trace even a slight snag in the *sahitya*. We were all wondering, how were you able to compose in Sanskrit? How did you get the proficiency?" Murali replied, "I don't have any such proficiency, nor have I studied any work on the *lakshana*". Sastri continued, "A scrutiny of the compositions does not make me believe your words. Anyway, I have been commanded by Goddess Durga to teach you the *sahitya lakshana* so that, nobody could question your knowledge in the grammar of *sahitya*, anytime in the future. From today, I will be you *guru* for this". Right away, Sastri began the first lesson to his new *sishya*. The classes under Ayyappa Sastri truly benefitted Balamuralikrshna and enriched his composing talent. In the preface to his work, "Janka Raga Kriti Manjari", Balamuralikrshna has written:

"I pay my salutations to 'Satavadhani', 'Bandagarbha Kavi Samrat', Sri Bhamidipati Ayyappa Sastri, who with bountiful affections, has taught me the *lakshana* of poetry and Telugu *Sahitya*".

With the coaching by Ayyappa Sastri, Balamurali started to compose *Padyas*. Some Specimens are:

1. On Dasavatara:

Sree vasundagu devadevuni
sada chintinsu Prahaladunin
Devaraina Hiranyakasipudilan
dveshan badhimpaga

'Sreevasa nanugavu' manchu goluvan
Sree Narasimhundavi
Neevarakshakunin vidanchi sutunin
gavanagalede Prabhoo!

2. A *padya* from the bunch, 'Manasu Cheppina Mata', on the death of the Hrikatha exponent, Musunoori Sooryanarayana Bhagavatar:

Vinalemika a kathakuni
knaleduvanti Gayakamanini vruthvin
mana notlaru kalilo bahu
dinamulu sajjana chayambu trimaidnundee!

Balamuralikrshna wanted to compose the life history of Sri Tyagaraja in *Padya* form

Ka. *Sreemantambagu tanjapu*
ree mandalamadi Kaveree teeramunan
komala sasya samruddhi na-
bho mandala madhya Sooryuvolen varalun.

See. *Sree Rama namaika Chintanasaktundu*
Tyagaraju dviteeyatmajundu
pinna Vayasunante Vedanta sarambu
paramartha chintayun barandelise.

This *Padya* series has not been completed. Sanskrit or Telugu, English or Tamil, singing or playing on the musical instruments or composing *kritis* or music — be what it may — the excellence Balamurali achieved, could not be attributed to the learning and catechistic sessions he had under his *guru* (or *gurus*) or by any studious efforts of his. This versatility of high calibre was nothing but a 'God-given' endowment.

"Janka Raga Kriti Manjari", containing the seventy two *melaraga kritis* of Balamuralikrshna, in the original Telugu script, was released on 27.9.1952, in the Durgapuram temple, where he made his debut about twelve years ago. He had actually completed all the seventy two, before 1948, but got them printed and published only four years later. The function was presided over by 'Kavi Samrat' Viswanatha Sathayanarayana. 'Avadhana Siromani' Kasi Krshancharyulu has written vividly about the brilliant compositions of Balamurali in his forward to this work. An extract:

"Chiranjeevi Mangalampalli Balamuralikrshna has done a yeoman service to the world of music.... It is distinctly clear that these *kritis* are in the style of Tyagaraja's compositions. When people are trying to get rid of the Sanskrit language, wrongly thinking that it is very difficult to pronounce it rightly, Balamurali has created many compositions in simple and easy Sanskrit. Perhaps, it is the 'Balamuralikrshna of Brundavan' who has fused the ability to this Balamuralikrshna..... I very strongly believe that Sri Tyagaraja's *amsa* is evident in our Balamuralikrshna".

Pingali Lakshmikanta Kavi, by a letter, expressed his appreciation that like music, the talent to compose has also been inherited by Balamuralikrshna, in this birth itself. "Janaka Raga Kriti Manjari" was dedicated to Goddess Kanakadurgadevi, the presiding deity of Durgapuram. This work is a golden treasury to the world of music. Having come to know that Balamurali has done a work, which was not so-far attempted by any other musician of Andhra Pradesh, the institution, "Andhra Saraswata parishad" resolved to honour him, A function was arranged in February, 1952, even when the book was still in the press to confer on Balamuralikrshna, the title of "Geeta Kala Bharati". The same *parishad* had already awarded him the title, "Gana Sudhakara". "Kavi Kathaka Ratnam". Peddinti Sooryanarayana Bhagavatar spoke highly about Balamuralikrshna and honoured him with another title, "Sahaja Vaggeyakara Ratnam".

Besides these seventytwo, Balamuralikrshna has composed hundreds of other compositions. It would be only a futile task to enumerate the songs tuned by him. I shall talk about them later.

M. Balamuralikrshna

Sri Parupalli Ramakrshnayya Pantulu, Guru of M. Balamuralikrshna

Smt. Sooryakantamma, mother of M. Balamuralikrshna

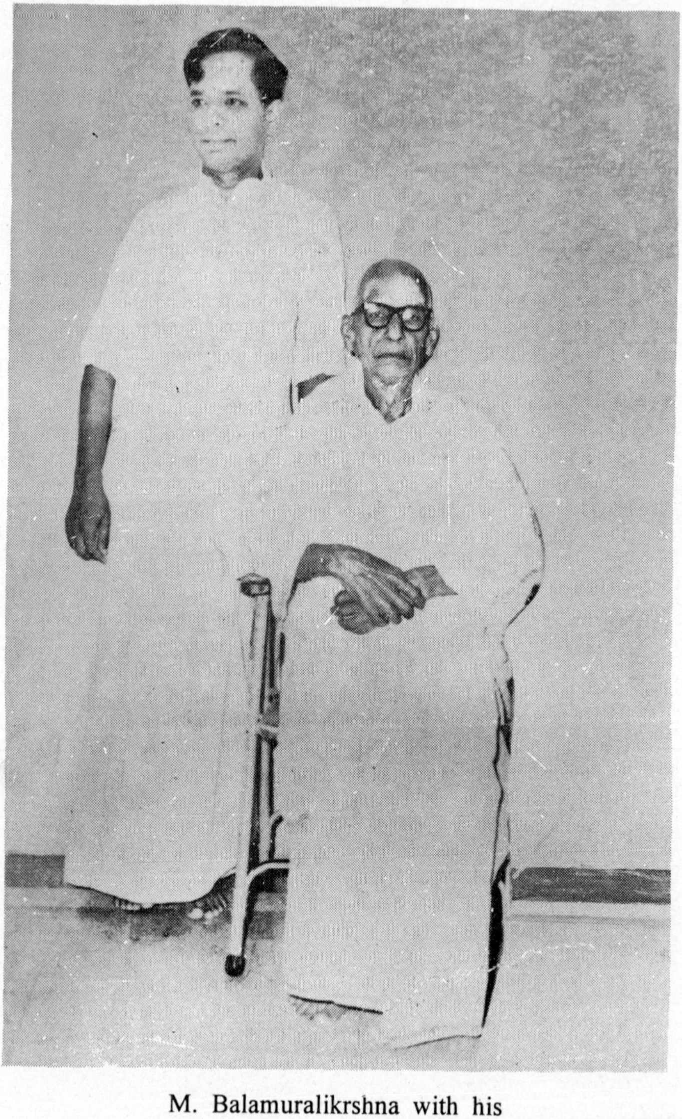

M. Balamuralikrshna with his father, Sri M. Pattabhiramayya

Balamuralikrshna in the Malyalam movie, 'Sandine Kendina Sindooram' as an old musician

Balamuralikrshna's first performance in Vijaywada

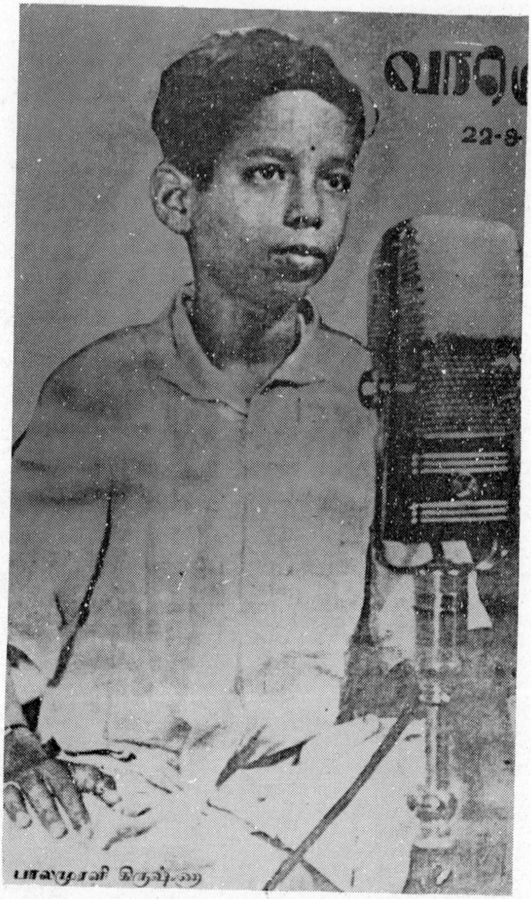

M. Balamuralikrshna's vocal broadcast from AIR, Madras on 22.8.1942.

Lata Mangeshkar and M. Balamuralikrshna

M. Balamuralikrshna with Sri V.V. Giri, the then President of India.

Mrs. Annapoorna Balamuralikrshna

M. Balamuralikrshna with Sri R. Venkataraman, the then President of India.

Madam's Arrival and After

Balamuralikrshna attained the age of thirteen. Since it was already late, Subbamma instigated Pattabhiramayya to perform the Upanayana (sacred thread wearing ceremony) for Murali. Pattabhiramayya was himself investitured with the sacred thread, at the age of eight. To postpone the Upanayanam of the boy further would not be proper. After consulting Parupalli and Sarabhayya, the date was fixed as 14.2.1944. Though the function was for one day, the celebrations extended upto eighteenth. The paper, "Andhra Prabha" carried a report on this, an extract from which is given below:-

"The Upanayanam of "Gana Sudhakara" Mangalampalli Balamuralikrshna, the famous musician, was celebrated as a big festival from fourteenth to eighteenth of February in Satyanarayanapuram, Vijayawada. 'Nagaswara Kovida' Deliparti Pichaharai brothers gave *nagaswara* recital at February 5.30 p.m. on fourteenth. Next morning 'Gayaka Ratnam' Musunoori Sooryanarayana Bhagavatar's Katha Kalakshepa was on the subject, "Krshna, an envoy of the Pandavas". The same evening, 'Gayaka Sarvabhouma' Parupalli Ramakrshnayya Pantulu gave a vocal recital. A vocal performance by Vankadari Venkatasubbayya Gupta was held on Sixteenth. A *veena* recital by Khambampati Akkaji Rao on the next morning and another vocal performance by 'Gayaka Ratnam' Chilakalapudi Venkateswara Sarma, that evening and at 9.30 p.m. a Katha Kalakshepa performance by 'Harikatha Ratnam' Peddinti Sooryanarayana Bhagavatar were also featured as a sumptuous feast for all the invitees. Everyone blessed the boy".

Now as Balamuralikrshna stepped into 'Brhmacharya Asrama'. the whole house was abuzz even a month after the function. The present status of Pattabhiramayya made some relatives happy, while some, within their hearts, envied him. Still others thought that it was their right to stay there and enjoy the hospitality, as long as they wanted. One of the well wishers of the family, during an informal chat, opened a new topic:

"Pattabhiramayya! Upanayanam is over. What is the use of being silent? I am sure you won't reject the hand of my daughter for your son". Soon, many others approached in similar ways. One relative said, "I shall give you rich dowry and other presents. There is no hurry. Whenever you think of getting Murali married, don't forget my daughter". Those who passed vituperative remarks and deriding comments on Pattabhiramayya, when he moved from place to place, in pursuit of learning music were now ready to give their daughters in marriage. Some who used to close their ears, even when the word 'music' was uttered, were now ready to make Murali, a musician, their son-in-law. While this was going on in the main hall, Subbamma was not spared by the womenfolk, inside the kitchen.

Horoscopes from relatives and others came in. Veluri Chandrasekharam, a nephew of Pattabhiramayya, who lived in Bhimavaram, came to his uncle and suggested the daughter of Prayaga Venkataratnam of Vissakoderu, a village about four kilometers away form Bhimavaram. He described the girl, Annapoorna, as beautiful, modest, soft-spoken and possessing all virtues. Venkataratnam was a prominent figure in that village and a distant relative of Pattabhiramayya. During his next trip to Vijayawada, Chandrasekharam landed at "Sooryakantam

Bhavanam" with Venkataratnam and some of his relatives. After a brief discussion on the subject, Chandrasekharam and Venkataratnam insisted that Pattabhiramayya should see the girl. Pattabhiramayya was against taking any dowry. His only condition was that the wedding should be celebrated for five days and Venkataratnam happily agreed. Prayaga Venkataratnam's daughter was engaged to Murali and the betrothal performed.

The wedding of Balamuralikrshna with Annapoorna took place on 14.3.1948 which was a Sunday, in a grand manner. Kasi Krshnacharyulu supervised the Vedic rituals while Parupalli Ramakrshnayya Pantulu took charge of the music programmes.

When the marriage party got back to Vijayawada on nineteenth, the altruistic Bethapudi Veera Sarabhayya, as per the earlier understanding that the new couple should place their first step only in his house, received everyone. He arranged for guests' luxurious feast for all. He celebrated as it were his own son's marriage with pomp and gaiety. Next day, Balamuralikrshna and the fourteen year old Annapoorna entered "Sooryakanta Bhavanam". Pattabhiramayya felt Annapoorna's coming had brought a new luster to the house. Subbamma was very happy and confident that her daughter-in-law would soon be able to lessen her own burden in managing the household. Balamurali never had any preconceived idea about how his wife should be. He had neither time nor any inclination to imagine all that. As days passed, he realized that Annapoorna was a personification of tolerance and was generous at heart.

On her part, Annapoorna had also never dwelt on any dreams not built any castles in her mind, about her would-be husband. The elders decided and got her married. But, that was not all!

To marry a musician, that too, a very renowned one, who is adored throughout the country has its own hurdles. Most of the days in a month, he may be absent from the house. Sometimes, the wife has to pass testing times which challenge her possessive nature which is common to every wife. She has to learn that the only formula to win her husband would be 'endurance'!

Annapoorna was now in a new place and new environment. The relatives who used to come her father's house would not extend their stay for more than a week. But in this place the situation was otherwise. Relatives would camp for months together; very punctual to sit for their food and not doing any thing for the rest of the time. Disciples of her husband, besides the surging multitude of *rasikas* were daily visitors. Some had to be fed in her house, on a regular basis. She had also been tutored, when young, to some rudimentary lessons in music, but, by listening, she had cultivated a taste in that art and was able to appreciate good music. Here, she came across many women enamoured by the melodious voice of her husband, adulating him and hanging around. Very soon, Annapoorna proved herself to be a mass of pure gold, that comes out of the goldsmith's crucible.

The love and affection between Balamurulikrshna and his wife was mutual and they had six children, three boys and three girls. The eldest, being a daughter, Murali named her Durga Sooryakantam, after his mother. The second was named Abhiram, a short form of Pattabhiramayya's name. Lakshmi is the third one, Sudhakar, the fourth child is now a leading surgeon, having his own nursing home, at Madras. His next brother, Vamsee Mohan is also a doctor, practising along with Sudhakar. The last child is a girl, 'Mahati'. Mahati is the name of the *veena* in the hands of Sage Narada. Balamuralikrshna's bungalow at Madras, also bears this name. Perhaps, Balamurali has a great liking for this name, that he has given it to a new *raga*, invented by him, having only four *swaras*. Besides, he founded an institution with the name 'Mahati', at the request of some friends and produced a stage play, 'Tyagaraja', in which, he himself played the role of the saint composer.

Pattabhiramayya was beaming with joy. A son with name and fame: uninterrupted income; a worthy daughter-in-law; the joy of having (at that time) two grandchildren. Could there be any other more person lucky than Pattabhiramayya? Murali would not have earned such a enviable status, Pattabhyiramayya thought, except for the boy's discontinuance of schooling, thanks to the sane and timely advice of Puttaparti Narayanacharyulu. But destiny meant otherwise. This overwhelming joy of Pattabhiramayya did not last long. A day came when he had to repent for taking the boy out of school.

In 1951, a remarkable change in the voice of Balamuralikrshna was noticed. His original singing pitch was G, but now, he was unable to sing even in C. It is common to have a voice change during adolescence, but Murali got it at the age of twenty one. Real lovers of music and Balamurali's fans felt very sad over his state. What a beautiful voice he had? Would they be lucky anymore to hear the delectable melodies out of him? Some said, "We knew this already. He ought to have practiced regularly, atleast, for some years, instead starting to sing all of a sudden? There was no discipline in him". Some remarked, "All these years, was he not standing on his head? Now he has been shown the right place. His capacity to mint money in lakhs is gone with the wind. No question of seeing a pie, anymore. Only till the boy had a euphonious voice was he able to do that and now the chapter has come to an end". A pall of gloom descended on Pattabhiramayya. The impresarios had started to cancel Balamurali's concerts; in some case, he himself regretted his inability through telegrams. It was a grave mistake that the schooling was discontinued. Otherwise, the boy would have become a graduate by then and secured a job, with a regular monthly salary in some government office. Even now a private teacher could be engaged, but would Murali bend himself to sit and study? Was he ever attentive in his music classes? Only because of God's grace, music started to flow from him. To get a job seemed to be out of question. Even connected with music, something like a music teacher in any school, one has to produce certificates. In fact, they go only by the certificates, rather than by merit, those days. But Subbamma was very confident that the boy's present ailment was only temporary and the day when people would be crazy to hear his voice was not far off. From inside the room, Balamurali was overhearing the conversation between Subbamma and Pattabhiramayya. Darkness engulfed not only his heart but also the place, as night settled in.

The rays of the rising sun peeped into the room. Balamurali woke up, as if a hope dawned and quickly finishing his morning ablutions, set out. Nobody knew whereto and why.

The children ran into a room and joyously shouted, "Daddy! Balamuralikrshnagaru has come". It was the house of Dr. Ayyagari Veerabhadra Rao, the then Station Director of All India Radio, Vijayawada. He was a devout *rasika* of Balamurali's music. He hurried out of the room, welcomed the star and after an exchange of pleasantries enquired what brought Murali to his house, at such an early hour. The conversation went on:

Murali: I have come here seeking help from you. Please assure me that you won't refuse me.

Rao: I shall certainly do anything for you, provided I can. Tell me, What help do you want?

Murali: I don't know how you will do it, but immediately I want a job. It is enough if I get two hundred, a month.

Rao: Job? For you? Why? We people have no other alternative but to undertake an employment, which is not so in your case. As a great musician, you can happily sit on a sofa, cross-legged, and people would come and shower wealth on you. You are independent. Why do you want a job, in which you have to be accountable to any Tom and Dick who doesn't know what music is?

Murali: Now things are changed. My voice is not as it was before. Already I am a father of two children. Unless you show me a way, by securing some job, be it what may, I do not know what would happen to me.

Rao: Oh! You are worried about the change in your voice. But bear my words well in your mind. The voice you possessed so far is not your natural one. Wait and see. How many lakhs of people are going to be enraptured by your natural voice, which you will get soon. This is only a stage. As days pass you will become alright, nay, you will get a more melodious voice. Remember my words on that day. Anyway, you want a job now. You are not a degree-holder. What type of job could I search for you?... Ok... leave it to me and give some time.

Taking leave of him, Balamuralikrshna returned to his house, looking pensive and crest-fallen. Two months after the above incident, he got a letter. The content was that the Director General of All India Radio was pleased to appoint Mangalampalli Balamuralikrshna as Music Superviser in the Vijayawada Station of All India Radio, with effect from 14 March, 1952. The enclosure was a monthly contract, mentioning Rupees two hundred and fifty, as salary. Pattabhiramayya flew in the air full of joy, not because his son had got a job, but because it came through the boy's own effort.

Annapoorna was reminded of an earlier incident. Once she was travelling on a train from Vijayawada, on her way to her native place. Sarada, her old school-mate was also in the same coach. In the course of their conversation Sarada said, with a sort of derision, "Oh! Your husband is a musician? I thought he would be some officer. I have four children. Though we have music instructor for them in Hyderabad, where we live, he is not good and regular. In one or two months, we are going to shift our residence to Vijayawada, on a transfer of my husband. I will then contact you. It is for you to put a word to your husband and arrange for him to teach music to my children". How humiliating were these words to Annapoorna! Many came to her husband, to learn music, but he was not an ordinary music teacher, like anyone else. Today, the scene had changed. Now she was also the wife of a respectable Government Officer.

Dr. Veerabhadra Rao started to brood over, on the day of Balamurali's visit this house. What job could he get for Murali? It would be good, he decided if such an employment is in All India Radio, so that the organisation would be richly benefitted. He wrote to the Directorate at Delhi about the merits of Balamurali, with a request, to give him a job and not to give cognizance to his age or any certificate in the art. After some days, he himself went to Delhi and personally put a word to the Director-General. He stressed that AIR should not fail to utilise the services of such a knowledgeable artist. The higher authorities were convinced and accepted Dr. Rao's plea and asked him to appoint Balamuralikrshna, forthwith. On his return from Delhi, Dr. Rao sent for Murali and conveyed to him the happy tidings, but asked him to be silent, till he received the official communication. Balamuralikrshna signed the contract for the post of Music Superviser on 14.3.1952 (Telugu New Year's Day) and despatched it with a request, that he may be permitted to join duty on 1st April.

At the same period, Swami Vimalananda Bharati came to Vijayawada, after his sojourn in the North. As was usual, he sent for Balamurali and asked him to sing in praise of the Goddess. With eyes drenched with tears, Murali humbly submitted his inability to sing. The omniscient Swamiji said, "What is this? What a simpleton you are? Even the Goddess Herself will not accept that a divine musician has lost his voice. Come on! Leave it to Her and start singing". Murali gently tried and slowly he was able to sing, though not in the form as before. Swamiji blessed him with the words, "Don't be dejected. You will very soon get a good voice, by Her grace. It was only She, who sent you to this earth and She knows that the very purpose of Your *Avatara* has not yet started. Good Luck". There was an improvement in Balamuralikirshna's voice gradually and it soon became very favourable.

The standard of the music programmes broadcast from AIR, Vijayawada, rose to heights, after the new Music Superviser took charge. Sometime later, Dr. Rao proposed to Delhi that a light music section could be started in his station. On a green signal form the mandarins at Delhi, he appointed Balamurali as music producer, with additional charge of Devotional music. The salary was also enhanced to four hundred and fifty. Later similar posts were created at other stations also.

Balamuralikrshna, for the first time, introduced a new programme, entitled "Bhakti Ranjani". It is purely a devotional programme, Adhyatma Ramayana Keertanas, Sadasiva Brahmendra Keertanas, Jayadeva Ashtapadis, Narayana Teertha Tarangams, songs of Bhadrachalam Ramadasa, Tumu Narasimhadasa, Annamacharya and many others got a facelift, with the tunes of Balamuralikrshna. It placed a feather on the cap of AIR, Vijayawada. Even today, this programme is very popular and is listened to by thousands, every morning, from even outside that state, thanks to the efforts of Balamuralikrshna. Later, other stations followed suit. In the meantime, Balamurali regained his sonorous voice, sweeter than earlier. Melody, fluency to execute any phrase at an incredible speed with felicity - everything he regained, by the grace of God. As a Dr. Veerabhadra Rao and Subbamma prophesied, multitude of invitations for concerts began to arrive. In 1956, Balamuralikrshna was transferred to Madras. He assumed charge at Madras, where he once, as a young boy, used to broadcast. Many rich persons and *rasikas* became his friends, during his tenure there. Two years after, he was again transferred to Hyderabad. Balamurali used to say, "This is the trouble with government service. Even before a year passed, after my joining duty at Hyderabad, I was once again transferred to Vijayawada. In fact, I was searching for a suitable house at Hyderabad, to settle my family there, but there was no necessity for that, because of this transfer. These transfers not only affected my family, but also my career. I had to lose a number of concerts, because of my government service and transfers".

His joining in the service of All India Radio, offered him a regular salary; he earned an indelible name for the introduction of "Bhakti Ranjani" programme. The year, he regained his voice. Dr. Rajendra Prasad, the then President of India, honoured Balamuralikrshna with a Gold Medal in the year 1953. The awardee was only twenty three years of age then and the youngest artist to get the honour. Not only that he was the first vocalist from Andhra Pradesh to get the President's Gold Medal.

When Balamuralikrshna returned to Vijayawada, after this national honour, Bethapudi Veera Sarabhayya drenched him with hundred baskets of flowers, on the railway platform itself. Balamuralikrshna used to say often, "His love and encouragement was ever bountiful; I am very much beholden to him, throughout this life".

Damodaram Sanjeevayya was the Chief Minister of Andhra Pradesh. On his suggestion, the Government planned to open a Music College at Vijayawada. A panel was constituted to select a fitting musician to the post of Principal. The panel, after deep consultation, decided that Balamuralikrshna, an outstanding musician, who could wield many instruments, who possessed abundant knowledge, who could teach the students in an able manner and who had a rich experience in administration, by virtue of his office in All India Radio, was the fittest person to head the institution. There were also some, who inspite of being close to Balamuralikrshna did not hesitate to write anonymous letters to the Government that Balamurali had not even completed sixth standard in school education and he possessed not even the basic qualifications to steer a Music College. But the Government did not give any credence to all this. It wrote to Balamuralikrshna, requesting his willingness to take up the new assignment and also to suggest a name for the college. Because of his travails in the service of All India Radio, he thought it was high time to quit it and accept the new offer. He had to resign his lucrative post in the central government service. Accepting the offer, he suggested that the college may deservingly be named after his *guru*, Parupalli Ramakrshnayya Pantulu. He met some high officials in the Government and persuaded them to name the college, according to his suggestion. The Education Ministry wrote to him that, for the time being, the college would function as "Government College of Music and Dance" and his proposal would be carried out soon. The college was inaugurated. Balamuralikrshna, after relinquishing his post in All India Radio, took charge on 1 April, 1960 as the first principal of this Government Music College. The present post, as a Gazetted officer, was prestigious and by that he could train many and make them expert musicians. That was his ambition. Otherwise, why should he give up a Central Government job and take up one that fetched much lesser salary than what he was drawing in AIR? He appointed as lecturers those, whom he considered would assist him, in achieving his goal. He made the environment to be beautiful and serene; various musical instruments were purchased for use, at a cost of twenty five thousand rupees; a five year course was introduced day and night. He devoted much of his precious time for the improvement of the college. But unfortunately, his enthusiasm started to dwindle. The Government, whom Balamurali expected would be conducive to these developmental measures, turned hostile. Trouble started brewing, when it put restrictions in appointing the teaching staff. As with other courses like Science, Medicine etc., it passed strictures that only degree-holders would be eligible for appointment. Balamuralikrshna dashed off letters to all those who matter, explaining in detail that music is not one like any other art or science and only persons with ripe experience, though not graduates, would be fit enough to teach this particular art. There is no doubt that reforms are imperative at all levels and on many occasions. However, there are certain core areas — particularly in a music college — where certain considerations are necessary, if the institution is to succeed in producing talented musicians and musicologists. Any change would vitiate the academic life and smooth functioning of the institution. But all went into deaf ears. The college fell in the throes of a crisis and made him chagrined.

The Principal is the pivotal person in a college. He is the adiminstrator, academic leader, friend, philosopher and guide to the institution's community comprising teachers, students, non-teaching staff, parents and the society at large. In fact an educational institution is what its Principal makes it to be. Balamuralikrshna was left practically with no time and motivation to deal with his broad areas of responsibilities. The Government officials persistently called for explanation, for even a petty thing done by him. They also accused him with the charge that he had appointed inexperienced youngsters and that he had wasted public money, as he pleased. The individuals appointed earlier by Balamuralikrshna were terminated from service, while some undeserving persons were promoted! Restrictions to accept concert engagements were imposed on the Principal. The sudden eruption of the trouble was more due to personal likes and dislikes of some top brass in the political arena. One or two students of his, as well as, some among those appointed by him, had also a considerable share in this scurrilous abetment to Government. Senior members of the teaching faculty did not join hands with those ungrateful ones, to antagonise Balamuralikrshna and thereby to jeopardise the student community. Troubled by all this, he tried managing to the best of his abilities A change in the musical items for the curriculum was brought into effect, without the knowledge of the Principal. Balamuralikrshna is a person, who could tolerate any insolence cast at him, but not to music, the art he always worships as divine. Mental agony was at a peak. He wanted to get out of the situation and the only option was to resign from his post, before the completion of three year tenure in office. He dispatched his resignation letter on 30.1.1963 and decided to quit the next day.

Next afternoon, I was sitting in the foyer of the college building. My *guruji*, Balamuralikrshna was handing over the charge, sitting in his room, to one of his colleagues. The peon brought a telegram, addressed to my *guruji* and handed it over to me. I took it inside; Balamuralikrshna opened it and I noticed tears in his eyes. I got perturbed, as to what could be the matter.

He passed on the telegram to me and signalled me to read it. The message was:

"Appointed as Music Producer AIR Madras Join duty forthwith.

— B. Gopala Reddy"

Dr. Bezawada Gopala Reddy is a connoisseur of music as well as a fan and well-wisher of Balamuralikrshna. At that time, he was the Union Minister for Information and Broadcasting. For quite some time, he was aware, how the Andhra Government was torturing Balamurali, a man of prestige, with independent attitude. But Dr. Reddy did not know about his resignation. The resignation letter was sent only a day earlier to the Education Secretary of the Government and the telegram from Dr. Reddy was just a coincidence, but relieved Balamurali's anguish. He came out of the college happily, brushing aside the whole episode about the college, as merely a dream. The Music College had later been named after Ghantasala Venkateswara Rao, a famous cine playback singer and Music Director.

Balamuralikrshna did not want to stay at Vijayawada any longer. After deciding to bring his family later to Madras, he, accompanied by me came to Madras and assumed office as the music producer, on the first day of February, 1963. All the friends and fans at Madras, extended him a warm welcome. Well-wishers compelled him to settle down there, the seat of Carnatic music and he then and there resolved to become "the son of the soil". One elderly musician told him, "the capital should not be without the king". Balamuralikrshna's family arrived about three months later and a house in Venkatachala Mudali Street, Mylapore was rented, temporarily. He did not relish living in a rented house and so we went around, in search of a good house for purchase. At last, a newly built bungalow in the colony, called Kanakasri Nagar, adjacent to the Madras Music Academy building was bought. Balamuralikrshna named it 'Mahati' and performed the *Grahapravesam* on 28.5.1964.

Pattabhairamayya and Subbamma were not happy

over Balamurali's bidding farewell to Vijayawada. They wanted him to come back, but, Balamuralikrshna alienated himself from Andhra Pradesh and became *Madrasi*. In the beginning, Pattabhiramayya was reluctant to move out of Vijayawada. He joined his son's family, later. The only individual whe was unyielding to their request was Subbamma. When compelled to come to Madras, she would say, "Who is to lookafter all these? Is it not necessary that someone should be here? Let them live in Madras or anywhere they like. I won't come. It is more than thirty years, since I placed my steps in Vijayawada, with the child. I want to die only here, on the banks of the river, Krshna".

The Music Producer's post, though, a timely help, was not a bed of roses. He was happy with the excellent programmes, he produced and it was reasonable as far as job satisfaction was concerned. But he had to often taste bitterness with regard to the official red tape. Going outstations for concerts was not an easy affair. He had to obtain prior written permission every time, to do so. Moreover, if away for a longer period, say twenty days a month, due to series of concerts, he had to forego his salary for the days of his absence. Some friends were, at that time, inviting him to come overseas, on a concert tour. Getting a 'No Objection Certificate' from All India Radio's headquarters would be possible, only after undergoing a number of formalities which were very cumbersome. His position as a 'most sought after' performing musician deprived him from doing full justice to his job. His official work soon became perfunctory. Thinking that he would perhaps discharge his duties more zealously if he had been placed out of Madras, the Directorate transferred him to Hyderabad. His representations to the authorities to retain him at Madras itself, since he had settled down with the family there, were turned down. He was in a doldrum, as to what to do next. Already he had decided not to live in Andhra Pradesh anymore. He was caught in a dilemma. Finally, Balamuralikrshna resigned willy-nilly his job in September, 1964 and became a free bird. The fetters that were binding him, for about two years, shattered now to pieces. The words of Dr. Veerabhadra Rao came to his mind. Yes! Hereafter he need not answer anyone except to God. What a great man, Dr. Rao! Could he not enthrall the entire world by the ambrosia of his music? Balamurlikrshna always cherishes in the core of his heart, Swami Vimalananda Bharati and Dr. Ayyagari Veerabhadra Rao.

Once Balamuralikrshna had been to Delhi for some concerts. On return, he got down in Vijayawada, without any prior intention, although he had a ticket to Madras. He was taken aback to see many people in his house. He entered and became overcome to see his 'mother' lying on the bed. Pattabhiramayya was already there, on a message from the tenant living downstairs. Subbamma was indisposed and had not moved out from the house, for the past four or five days. Balamurali planned to take her to Madras immediately and give her the best medical treatment, at any cost. But the neighbors said, it was not advisable, since her condition was not favourable to undertake a travel. Subbamma, who was unconscious all along, opened her eyes slightly, perhaps because the voice of her affectionate son fell on her ears. She looked at him for some minutes and then gesticulated that she wanted water. Balamurali brought water and poured it in her mouth. He requested his father and others to lookafter her and hurried to Madras, by flight, to bring his wife and children to Vijayawada. Unfortunately, when he stepped into his house, he recieved a telegram, carrying the news that Subbamma had attained the feet of God. His grief was beyond description. He had not seen his mother's face. The only mother knew he was Subbamma. May be, it was only her affection and desire to see for the last time her son, whom she had lovingly nurtured and brought up, made Balamurali, intutionally, to get down at Vijayawada. His cries rent the air. Pattabhiramayya's sobs continued for long hours. The big banyan tree. which sheltered him and his son, was now fallen. As desired by Subbamma, her funeral rites were performed on the banks of the rivser Krshna.

Subbamma, the only relative, who remained in Vijayawada was now no more and Balamurlikrshna became resolute in cutting off his ties with the place, except that he owns "Sooryakanta Bhavanam", there. For a long time the painful memory always seemed to be there, sitting on the edge of his consciousness, waiting to bring back the pain he only wanted to forget.

Balamurlikrshna undertook a concert tour to Sri Lanka in 1967 and cast a spell over the lovers of music in that country. This was his first foreign visit.

Paramountcy Conquered

Many came to him from Andhra Pradesh, Tamilnadu, Kerala and Karnataka and some other North Indian States, to study music. Most of them, staying somewhere, on their own arrangement, used to come in the morning or evening for the classes. I am proud to mention here that I am his first student from Tamilnadu and that too, in the 'Gurukulavasa' system. My boarding and accommodation were in his house itself. That period between 1957 and 1963, I consider to be the most precious in my life. I lived with him, day and night and learnt under his feet. Regular classes were there, either in the morning or in the evening. We would usually relax, during the early nights, sitting and chatting in the open terrace of his house (both in Vijayawada and at Madras). That was the hour, when he would take up some topic on music and musicology and conduct a class informally. Sometimes, the subject would be of a general nature. He had already known to converse in Tamil, with a Telugu slang, he could speak but not read and write Tamil. I used to enjoy his Teluguised Tamil and he would also join in the peels of laughter. On one such session, the topic turned towards the Tamil language. His interest in knowing to read and write in Tamil was keen that he asked me to write the alphabets on a sheet of paper. When I did so and explained what is what, he threw away the paper, saying that he felt it was difficult. Then we spoke about something else and retired to bed. The next morning, when I got up, I saw he was deeply engaged in writing something. I moved away not wanting to disturb him. He beckoned and showed me the paper. I was simply dumbfounded. It was a letter in Tamil! How was he able to do it? Because, only the previous night he said it would be difficult to go through the alphabet. For the preceding five or six years and until the previous day, it was my duty to read for him the letters in Tamil, he received from various places of Tamilnadu and to reply to them, on his behalf. Now I understood my services in this regard may not be required, any more. He solved the mystery:

"For a long time, my deficiency in Tamil was worrying me. Yesterday also, we were discussing about it. After my usual prayer to Maruti, with my worry embedded in the mind, I went to bed and soon fell in a dream! An old man approached me and requested me to help him by writing what he dictated in Tamil. When I expressed my inability, he pestered me by saying, 'if you don't want to help me, that is different. But don't tell a lie. I know you can write very well in Tamil. Please try not to evade'. I was forced to lay my hand on the paper and I don't know how, but I completed it, to my own surprise. Thanking me he left. That's all. I immediately woke up to understand that it was only a dream. With a curiosity to test, I ventured to try writing again and this short letter is the result".

He had come out of the dream, pushing me into it! Balamuralikrshna's achievements are many folded, not easily initiated by others. The above incidence is only an other of them. He was inspired to compose many songs in Tamil, for a concert repertoire.

In Tiruvaiyaru, the birth-place of the great composer, Sri Tyagaraja, an organisation came up with the name, "Tamil Isai Iyakkam" about two decades ago. Its sole aim was to foster and give importance to Tamil songs. Barring one or two, all other musicians, who participate in this organisation's annual festival, never sing exclusively

Tamil songs. One or two compositions of Tyagaraja always find a place, without fail. When Balamuralikrshna was invited to give a concert there in 1976, the eyebrows of many stood up. What? Balamurali in a Tamil Isai festival? Not a digestible thing. It is needless to say that his performance there consisted only of Tamil songs, from the beginning to the end. It took everyone by surprise. Some individuals came near him, at the close of the recital, and expressed their view that since Tiruvaiyaru is a place sanctified by Tyagaraja, had his songs also been rendered, it would have been a mark of devotion to such a great saint — composer. Balamuralikrshna chuckled and turning towards me said, "They think that only by singing Tyagaraja's songs, I could exhibit my devotion to him. Can anyone assert that singing them even in his Aradhana Festival would be based only on devotion? No other songs are permitted in this festival and therefore, we should not sing here, in any other language". There could not be even a single *rasika*, who had not tasted his delectable compositions in Tamil. *Pirai aniyum Preuman* (Hamsadhwani), *Aya Kalaikkellam* (Mohanam), *Tunai Neeya Kumara* (Charukesi) and *Varuga Varuga Mamayileriye* (Pantuvarali) may be cited as few specimens. His virtuosity and the boundless appeal of his music brook no barrier.

He first took up composing *kritis* in the Seventy two *melaragas*, and then a number of compositions in Telugu, Sanskrit and Tamil, in *Janyaragas*. We shall discus the new *ragas* created by him, later. Whenever he is mentally inspired, a new song would take its birth. In this regard, I would like to narrate some personal experiences.

We had to go to Srirangam, after a concert by Balamurlikrshna at Kumbakonam. In between, there was a day's rest and so we went to Tanjavur, my native place. Two of his other disciples — the late, M.V. Ramanamurthi and M. Chittaranjan of Hyderabad, were also there. We visited the Bruhadeesware temple, where the priest requested our *guruji* to sing a song. Balamuralikrshna instead asked us to sing. Ramanamurthi and Chittaranjan rendered the *kriti* 'Siva Siva', at the shrine of the presiding deity. In front of the Goddess, Bruhannayaki, Ramana murthi sang 'Nee Dayarada' in the *raga*, Poorvikalyani, a composition of our *guruji*. Then we circumambulated the Prakara. Within that time, Balamuralikrshna mentally composed a song. He took us again to the main shrine and delivered his new composition, 'Bruhadeeswara Mahadeva' (Kanada Roopaka), which is a brilliant composition in that *raga* and soon became very popular. Similarly, 'Doravadari Vacchidiva' in Natakuringi *raga* was composed at the shrine of Lord Krshna, at Guruvayur, 'Ganamalinchi' (Kalyanavasantam) at Madurai, the Neelambari piece, 'Bangaru Murali' at Udupi and 'Kavave Kanyakumari' (Sahana) at Kanyakumari. The last named is the first Sahana composition set to Misra Chaputala, hitherto not available. I may go on citing such instances. When Balamurali visited Yadagiri in 1971, for a concert, he composed 'Margata Simhasana' in the *raga*, Simhendramadhyamam, in praise of the deity, Lakashminarasimha. Every song took birth giving expression to his creative impulse.

During one of the post-dinner sessions in the open terrace of his house, about which, mention has already been made, our *guruji* was humming the *raga* Kalyani and in about few minutes, emerged a new song, 'Sogasu Nee Sommu', with a novel tinge in the shades of the *raga*. Another song 'Nee mata na lona' in Seelangi was also born on one such occasion. Scarce were the days that he had no concert schedule. After his settlement at Madras, whenever he was free, we used to go to the beach and spend some hours in an uncrowded corner. At such times he would teach or explain some rare things in music. One day he introduced to us a new song of his, 'Talavari nisi'. It was so beautiful that I could not restrain my curiosity to know the name of the *raga*. He demonstrated the *swaras* both in the ascending and descending order, without naming the *raga*. It was pentatonic and more similar to Mohana *raga*, but the *rshabha* was with higher *sruti* value. There is an occasional touch also of the *Suddha Dhaivat* (Komal Dhaivat). I humbly suggested, it would be nice if he composed a *kriti*, in the same *raga*, because 'Talavari nisi' is a light song. The next evening, we were on the beach, facing the sea and surprisingly, our *guru* was reflective, for some minutes, as if in a meditative mood. Then he wrote on the sand with his forefinger, a song. It was the custom for us, the disciples, to always carry a small note-book and pen, so that we could, then and there, note down the songs he composed or taught. Now, he drew the note-book from me and scribbled on it, what he wrote on the sand. Thus was born the *kriti*, 'Nee namamuna Jeevamu'. He added colours to the tune, while singing it. The *raga* was the same in which 'Talavari nisi' came out and he named it 'Mohanangi'. On that day, he created not only a new composition, but a new *raga* also.

Balamuralikrshna has created (still continues to do so) hundreds of compositions which are valuable gems. Confluence of melody and lucid lyric are embedded in everyone of these. *Tanavarnas*, *Padavarnas*, *kritis*, *tillanas*, *padas* and *javalis* composed by him are more than three hundred. He has not left out any genre of composition in the Carnatic music repertoire. His *tanavarna*, 'Saraguna Gavumu' in Todi is unique. The *panchama swara* has got an omission in this. Besides, the 'ettugada' *sahitya* (something like a Charana in the *kriti*) has the beauty of 'Swarakshara' (echoism) usage. Similarly, in the same Todi *raga* (with the inclusion of the customary use of *panchama*) there is an exquisite composition of his, beginning with the words, 'Ma Manini'. The whole *kriti* is in the 'Swarakshara' form and a rare of its kind. Deciphering the meaning of the *sahitya* is also not much easy. I shall give here the *pallavi* and *charana*.

Pallavi : Ma manini nee dhamagani needha sarini gada

Charana : Sarigani dharimari gadha dharee
niga niga gani neemagani
Sama nigama garima gani.

His *Javali* 'Marulu Konnane' in Jhinjhoti is very popular.

Tillanas are compositions meant for brisk rendering and therefore should always be in medium or fast tempos. The is the norm, enunciated by the composers of the past and Balamuralikrshna's *tillanas* adhere to this. At the same time, it is not easy to render his *tillanas,* as one could do others. "Dheem na nata Dhirana" in Hindola *raga* is his first *tillana* composition. Every *tillana* of his is replete with something special, mixed with complexity, in a subtle form. It requires great skill to do justice to them, while rendering, for it would be like a formidable feat. His *tillana* in 'Taya Ragamalika' has no parallel. The *ragas* employed in this *tillana* are sounded by a modal shift of tone, similarly as in the case of the *pallavi,* which he sung in the Madras Music Academy. The first *raga* is Kalyani and by the 'Graha Bheda' method, each section of the *tillana* emerges in the *ragas* Sankarabharnam, Mohanam, Hindola and Darbari Kanada. His recent *tillana* is in 'Priya Ragamalika' consisting Gurupriya, Rasikapriya, Gayakapriya, Sunadapriya and Kharaharapriya. Five sections of this *tillana* are in Chaturasra *gati, tisra gati, misra gati, sankeerna gati* and *khanda gati,* respectively.

Some of his *tillanas* have been published, in his own handwriting. At the request of many *rasikas* and aspiring students of music, Balamurlikrshna has brought out his 'Janka Raga Kriti Manjari' (his seventy two *melaraga kritis*) and 'Murali Ravali', a work containing some of his compositions in the *janya ragas,* in Tamil script. As a *Vaggeyakara,* he is, no doubt, a paragon. New aesthetic paradigms have been given to Carnatic music by him.

To compose music for a lyric is an art, demanding profound talent. Mere musical knowledge is not sufficient. One should know the meaning of the song, the situation in which it was composed and the mood and idea of the lyricist. If a song should become popular, the tune should be catchy and also fitting to the content of the lyric. The tunes scored by Balamuralikrshna, to the songs of Annamacharya, Sadasiva Brahemndra, Jayadeva and such others are entrenched in the hearts of every listener. Bountiful dynamics of composing made him delve deeper in the ocean of music and weave many delectable musical fabrics. The listeners, are re-sensitised by these innovations. The so called die-hards once accused Balamuralikrshna, as having changed the traditional tunes and giving them a new garb in a lighter shade. This necessitates a short explanation here. It is not understood what they presume as 'traditional' tunes. It is a matter of doubt, whether they themselves know what it means. For instance, let us take the *Ashtapadis* of Jayadeva.

Jayadeva, born in Bengal, ascribed his work *Geeta Govindam* to Lord Jagannath of Puri, in Orissa. He employed the *ragas* that were in vogue during his own times and region. They travelled down the South through the pilgrims or the migrators. The Carnatic musicians of an early period gave a new musical robe to the songs, with *ragas* of their system. *Ashtapadis* gained currency among the Bhagavatars of the South Indian Bhajana tradition. The tunes handled by them and alleged to be the original or traditional, were composed by Tirumalairayanpathinam Ramaudu Bhagavatar, who lived only about seven decades ago. The songs have musically undergone many changes with different practitioners, at different periods of time. Since the original tunes, if at all Jayadeva had done any, have not been preserved with notation, no one can argue that the recent musical setting by Ramude Bhagavatar or someone else is the original. These older tunes available may be good in general, but in many cases, do not fit in with the meaning and mood of the song. For example, the *Ashtapadi*, 'Pravisa Radhe'. The *sakhi* asks Radha to go near Krshna and also prays the latter to bestow blessings on Radha. Can anyone say that the so-called 'traditional' tune reflects the mood? Only those, who are bereft of aesthetic sense, may come forward with any dry argument. It is beyond doubt that only because Balamuralikrshna furbished the *Ashtapadis* with a new form, a new color, most appropriate to the content, they became most popular and he was deservedly conferred with the title,

'Abhinava Jayadeva'. We are reminded of Pandit Jawaharlal Nehru's words: "Creative art must be allowed and encouraged to grow with as little interference as possible". Balamuralikrshna taught some of us, the art of composing music. He would often emphasise the necessity of knowing the meaning of the lyric and so on. Also he used to advise, "try to fuse any new and attractive innovation to the *raga* you choose, for the purpose". In the course, he would repeat the advice he got from his *guru*, Parupalli Ramakrshnayya Pantulu, (in his own words): "From what one learns from one's *guru*, one should with ones own intelligence and hardwork make a synthesis into something new. He must either consummate a tradition or initiate another, either do what has already been done in a better way or do something entirely new. There is no short cut for achieving greatness or fame in any art, and it is a very slow and difficult process which demands first of all proper training, intelligence and above all a long and sustained endeavour".

It is a great misfortune that the word 'tradition' is always mouthed by those, who neither know what 'tradition' really means, nor what 'non-tradition' is. The Sanskrit word for 'tradition' is said to be *Sampradaya*. *Sam* means 'good' 'refined' and *pradaya* means 'offering', that which is offered in a good refined or sophisticated manner is *sampradaya* and nothing more. A basic format in singing or composing or playing on an instrument, has been propounded by the ancients. For instance, a Varna is a musical form, comprising of a *pallavi, anupallavi, muktayiswara, ettugada* followed by sets of *swara* passages, called *Ettugada swaras*. This is tradition. The composer is at liberty to choose the *raga* and make out the *swara* phrases or *sahitya*, as he wants them to be. If only he changes the established order, he could be accused of being 'non-traditional'. Tradition, never rules out creativity. As such, it becomes obvious that the term 'tradition' is loosely used by most people.

A negligible section of the musical fraternity may feel that Balamuralikrshna's music is 'non-traditional'. There were number of stalwarts in the South Indian music field like Ariyakkudi Ramanuja Iyengar, Maharajapuram Viswanatha Iyer, Madurai Mani Iyer, G.N. Balasubramaniam and so on. None of them sang exactly like the other. Each one had devised an individual style and that is how they became celebrities. "I have never wanted to be a clone, to passively and soul-lessly reproduce another style. I have been able to evolve my own individual style" The characterisation of his art mainly lives in his stylistic innovation. It has virtually created a new awareness about the infinite potential of music. Some people are there who think Balamuralikrshna as ushering in some Hindustani *ragas* into Carnatic music. Who could says that Harikesanallur Muthayya Bhagavatar was not a Carnatic musician, but, it was he who introduced *ragas* like Gaud Malhar, Hamsanadi, Sohini, Mandand Jaunpur in the South? Was Gopalakrishna Bharati, the author of 'Nanda Charitram', not a Carnatic musician, since he learnt some lessons in Hindustani music from a North Indian singer, Ramdas and employed some *ragas* in his opera? The great Tyagaraja has composed some *keertanas* in Western airs, like 'Raminchuvaru', 'Varaleelaganalola' and so on. Is there anybody to level a charge of blasphemy against him? But, it is always common to speak ill of another or to be a cynic, when the critic himself could not achieve something. Every blame springs up from professional spite. *Sampradaya* never means 'stagnation'. There is a popular vocalist, who always would spilt the words in such a way, while rendering the *kriti*, which would tend to give some indecent meaning. When it was pointed out, he simply replied. "My *guru* sang only in this way and so I won't deviate from that tradition". Such are the advocates of 'tradition'! An extract from Balamuralikrshna's presidential address in the Madras Music Academy: "No doubt tradition is the basis of all human achievements. But the music should not become a museum piece by rigidly adhering to tradition alone. Tradition is the very substance from which one creates and progresses; but traditionalism is a barrier placed on progress in the name of what is obsolete. Change is however inevitable whether one likes it or not. Without invention there cannot be progress and therefore a judicious interplay of tradition and invention is necessary to develop good music. It is well known that the existing tradition of our Carnatic music is only the *sampradaya* of the recent past. One cannot sing or play as it was sung or played some hundred years ago or even fifty years back. Thus the concept of tradition is dynamic. Though tradition and change are opposite factors, the change is more powerful and influences tradition to change with the ages".

Music is for the enjoyment of the public. That is why, it is publicly distributed from the dais. If one says that music is meant for a chosen few, the very purpose of the art becomes nullified. It is quite interesting to note that those who are professionals, putting a veil on the term 'art', advocate that since music is divine, it is meant for a chosen few. If they believe what they say, they should confine music to some temple or to their own *pooja* room. Music on the platform is different. It becomes divine, if only it is catered to all, without any detriment to the established tenets of the system of music. Music's aim is to transform a philistine into a cultured one. Everyone ballyhoos in stentorian voices, that music is the easiest way to attain salvation. They cite Sri Tyagaraja's case, in support of it. True. Nobody can deny it. But how many, who practise music, would wish to leave this materially prosperous world, as easily and early as possible? Most of our musicians are very well aware that music, only in its pristine pure form could speed up *mukti*. May be due to the same reason, they are very happy that *mukti* is far-fetched for them.

There is another misgiving among musicians and music critics that Balamuralikrshna sings mostly his own compositions in his concerts. What is wrong in it? Is there any stipulation that one who creates a composition should not sing it himself? Is it that he has right only to compose but not to sing? If Tyagaraja had not sung his own compositions, in the course of his daily 'Unchavritti' or during his *pooja*. How could we have sung those today? Patnam Subramania Iyer, Ramanathapuram Shrinavasa Iyengar, Muthayya Bhagavatar and such others — did they not sing their own compositions in their programmes? G.N. Balasubramaniam, a musician cum-composer, also used to sing one or two of his compositions. If the composer himself does not sing, how could the compositions become popular? A composer, after bringing out a piece cannot rest contented and simply forget it. These compositions are for the public and should be sung of. As far as Balamuralikrshna is concerned, he never sings exclusively his own compositions in any of his concerts, unless so requested.

Deep musical experience is the main aim of a concert goer. Only a few musicians are capable of giving it, although, several of them have great technical accomplishments and larger repertoires than their predecessors. Balamurali's main aim is to make the *rasikas* attain their satisfaction.

Balamuralikrshna trailed a new blaze in his style of singing and composing with an individuality, which others cannot do or repeat. Nature has endowed him with enormous talent to innovate. His music may be deemed modern in its eclecticism and preoccupation with the abstract, but its mainsprings are to be found in the tradition. He is one, who mesmerises the lovers of music with his faultless and clear diction, may the lyric be in any language, embellished by pertinent articulations. The boundary between tradition and innovation becomes blurred in his hands. As J.S. Holland wrote, "Artists are nearest to God. Into their souls He breathes His life and from them it comes in fair, articulate forms to bless the world". It is true in the case of Balamuralikrshna, who has attained the pinnacles of glory, by swimming against the currant.

Sri Tyagabrahma Mahotsava Sabha, Tiruvaiyaru is a registered body to celebrate the Tyagaraja Aradhana Festival, annually. Only in 1906 the Aradhana Festival was commenced by two brothers, Tillaisthanam Narasimha Bhagavatar and Panju Bhagavatar. The very next year, they got separated, due to some misunderstanding, and conducted the festival, separately and at different places.

Those in allegiance with the elder, Narasimha Bhagavatar, were called the 'Priya Katchi' (elder's group) and the other as 'Chinna Katchi' (younger's group). When Bangalore Nagaratnamma entered the scene, she was taken aback to note that the concert platform was out of bounds to ladies in both the festivals, organised by the two factions. The world of Carnatic music, in the earlier part of this century, was beset by male chauvinism to a great extent. She felt women, not only as musicians but also as devotees of Tyagaraja, have a legitimate right to perform and offer their homage and there should not be any discrimination based on the gender. Since her requests to the organisers (of both groups) were not given heed to, she found no other alternative but to conduct another festival, exclusively for and by the ladies and this was called the 'Ladies' Group. Some influential well-wishers, observing such unhealthy trends in celebration of the Aradhana Festival, in the same village, by three groups, wanted to unify and mediated. Finally, all the groups came under one banner and thus the 'Tyagabrahma Mahotsava Sabha' came into existence and got registered. In 1940, the first festival by this Sabha was inaugurated by C. Rajagopalachari. Besides other office bearers, two secretaries are elected once in three years for the administration of the Sabha and to conduct the festival.

In 1962, after completing programme commitments in Paramakkudi and Rameswaram, Balamuralikrshna came to Tiruvaiyaru, with a desire to take part in the Tyagaraja festival. The then secretary refused to provide accommodation. He also curtly said that any musician, who wanted to participate should write well in advance, Balamurali's programme could thus not be arranged. This was the treatment meted by the secretary to Balamuralikrshna, who swept the whole audience by his enchanting music, just two decades ago. Some *rasikas*, who were there at that time, took the discomfitured Balamuralikrshna and his coterie to a vacant house, located in a nearby street and looked after all their comforts. "Tyagaraja, the great soul, is all-pervading and omnipresent. Not necessarily I should sing only there. My music would reach his ears, even if I sing from this place", said Balamurali. The news that he was going to perform in that house spread everywhere. There was no room for even slightest ventilation and not only the house, but the street itself was jam-packed. A portrait of Sri Tyagaraja was placed in the centre of the hall with oil-lamps lit in front of it. The reverberating melody sprung up from Balamuralikrshna and continued for about two hours. 'Evarito ne delpude Rama' a beautiful composition of Tyagaraja in the *raga*, Manavati, was quite fitting to the occasion and soul-stirring. Then he asked some of his disciples, who were with him (including me) to sing few songs. An hour before we started form Tiruvaiyaru, Balamuralikrshna went to the banks of the river Kaveri and composed a song on Tyagaraja, in the *raga*, Amrutavarshini "Samagana Sarvabhouma Swami Tyagaraja Nama". In the Charana, he says:

"Some are puffed up with arrogance thinking that they are greater than others. But all of us, exploit only your composition to acquire name, wealth, rich titles and so on. It is the idea of many that only they foster tradition and your real heirs. Please remove their megalomania and show them the righteous..." Yes! Tyagaraja showed it soon.

When we reached Tanjavur, Balamuralikrshna told me that he would not come again to Tiruvaiyaru, except in a proper manner. Perhaps these words might have reached the ears of Tyagaraja, that he decided to entrust the conduct of the festival itself to Balamuralikrshna. In 1972, his name was proposed for the post of secretary of the Tyagabrahma Mahotsava Sabha by the late, Tillaisthanam Vasudevan, the then treasurer, and was welcomed by all. He assumed the office on 1.4.1972 and came to Tiruvaiyaru in his new official capacity. His vow had borne the fruit. Balamuralikrshna made many improvements there. He introduced a life-membership scheme in order to accrue a corpus fund. He approached the Tirumalai-Tirupati devasthanam and requested to extend a helping hand, financially, to construct a building, where the partaking musicians could be lodged and got consent from the authorities to release rupees eight lakhs for the purpose. The Andhra Pradesh Government came forward and paid rupees two lakhs. It also assured that such grant may recur annually. Separate enclosure for boarding the musicians was arranged. Some musicians never stuck to time and went on singing, encroaching the next artiste's time. Many members suggested to Balamuralikrshna to instruct the man incharge of the public address system, to switch off the microphone, if anybody exceeded the allotted time slot. But Balamurali did not relish such and idea "poor ones! After all they are also musicians like us. Only over enthusiasm makes them unpunctual. Let's think about some other way", he said. In the next year he introduced the system of erection of two platforms, side by side, so that the musicians could occupy both stages, alternatively. While one is engaged, the other would be vacant and just a minute before the end of the ongoing concert, the other would be occupied and be ready by the next incumbent. This double-stage system, life membership scheme, programme book and many other things introduced by Dr. Balamuralikrshna are still in vogue.

Usually, after the choral singing of the *pancharatna kritis* are over, Nagaswara *vidwans* would commence to play, one after the other, till noon. On one such occasion, during the tenure of Balamuralikrshna's secretaryship, the nagaswara players resolved not to play during the aradhana rituals or in the procession of the Saint's portrait, for reasons known only to them. This reached the ears of the secretary. He asked all his disciples, who were there, to be ready. The *Pancharatna kritis* were over and as expected, there was not a single nagaswara player, to take over. All India Radio was relaying the event, direct and it had already announced that the relay would go upto 12 O'clock. Since there were no nagaswara *vidwans*, the officials got agitated. Not even slightly perturbed by all this, Balamuralikrshna signalled to all his disciples to sit around and himself started to sing the *Utsava Sampradaya Keertans* of Tyagaraja, each line repeated by the disciples in chorus. It was a grand feast to the listeners. Many of them wanted that this practice should be continued, also in the future. But Balamuralikrshna was not happy over such a suggestion, because it would deprive playing opportunities to the nagaswaram artists. The presence of mind and capability to manage difficult situations of Balamuralikrshna, became a matter of much discussion. In spite of his mutlivarious improvements and systematic organisation, Balamuralikrshna was driven to state that he did not want to continue in office. Observing the successful conduct of the festival with improvements added year after year, some mischief-mongers took to fissiparous efforts with the result, a misunderstanding crept in between Balamuralikrshna and a section of members. On the completion of a creditable tenure of two terms ending on 31.3.1978, Balamuralikrshna resigned. Even today, the way he conducted the Tyagaraja festival in a prestigious, impeccable, systematic and dignified manner is highly spoken of and many members of the Sabha, as well as musicians and *rasikas* say that "thet golden period of the Tyagaraja festival in the past four decades, was only when Balamuralikrshna was the secretary", thus though Balamuralikrshna wanted to bid a 'Good-bye' to Tiruvaiyaru, the wishes of Sri Tyagaraja were otherwise.

Bangalore Nagaratnamma endowed all her property to Tyagaraja, as said earlier. Some other devotees also donated their mite, by way of cash, house, shops and so on. Before her passing away, Nagaratnamma executed a will, by making the entire properties and assets including the samadhi premises and the lengthy yard in front of it (where the festival *shamiana* is erected every year, during the festival) as a Trust, named 'Vidya Sundari Bangalore Nagaratnamma Trust' (B.N.R. Trust). The Tyagabrahma Mahotsava Sabha or anyone else who wants to conduct any festival, should obtain prior permission from the Trust and nothing should be done detrimental to the sanctity of the premises, that come under the purview of the Trust. Three persons were nominated by Nagaratnamma as Trustees to celebrate the Aradhana

Festival or anything connected with the Trust, with an option of Managing Trustee, to look after the Trust, either single-handed or co-opting one or more Trustees. Atmaram Rao was the Managing Trustee, during the period 1976-1978 and for quite some time, he was thinking to include Balamuralikrshna, a real devotee of Sri Tyagaraja. When he came to know that Murali had resigned from the Tyagabrahma Mahotsava Sabha, he felt, it was the right time and invited him to become a Trustee. But, Balamuralikrshna had just then released a great sigh of relief and hence declined the invitation. Atmaram met him personally and tried to persuade him saying that it was only the divine command of Sri Tyagaraja otherwise, why should he go after Balamuralikrshna, when there were plenty of old-musicians, better known to him than Balamurali, available. Finally Atmaram Rao declared, "The lady bequeathed everything to *Swami*. When I wanted to relinquish this responsibility, due to old age, after entrusting it to some suitable and deserving person, it was only Nagaratanmma who appeared in my dream and suggested your name." As soon as the name of Nagaratnamma fell in the ears of Balamuralikrshna, he felt an electrifying experience. His memory rolled some decades back. How she blessed him! Did she not ask some swamiji also bless him? Did she not fetch him through a volunteer, as soon as his first performance was over in Tiruvaiyaru out of great interest in his music and his well-being? So, her command is nothing but a Divine command. After such thoughtful moments, Balamuralikrshna accepted. He was co-opted as a Trustee, by the only surviving Managing Trustee, Atmaram Rao, in the year 1978 - the same year in which Balamurali quit the post of the secretary from the Sabha. Two years later, Atmaram Rao resigned from the Trusteeship, due to indisposition and thereby Dr. Balamuralikrshna became the sole and Managing Trustee of the B.N.R. Trust.

Generally people visit the shrine of Sri Tyagaraja, only during the Aradhana Festival because they could have the *darshan* and enjoy music at the same time and naturally the *sannidhi* would be overflying with devotees and they have to wait for long to perform an *archana*. To avoid such congestion and also to help the priest to do every *archana* in a leasurely manner and individually for the benefit of every devotee, Balamuralikrshna devised a new scheme. Anyone who pays a prescribed amount to the Trust would get the *prasad*, after the performance of an *archana* on the day of the devotee's birth star, every year. By this, a considerable amount could flow into the Trust.

The Madras Music Academy is considered to be a prestigious institution in serving the cause of music. Its annual music festivals, conferences, Teachers College of Music, Publications, School of Bharatnatya and such other activities have won commendable honour and earned for it an international reputation. It is deemed to be the authority in matters of music and dance. The Executive Committee chooses some veteran artist to preside over the annual conference and to be bestowed its covetous title of 'Sangeeta Kalanidhi'. The selection is never done keeping in mind the age and seniority alone and the criteria is something more. Even the artists at a ripe age or popular or with vast experience are still in the waiting list. This committee in its meeting selected Dr. Balamuralikrshna for presiding over its annual conference and for the title of 'Sangeeta Kalanidhi'. It was matter of surprise to all, how knowledgeably and successfully Balamuralikrshna conducted the conference (1978-79) and many came to know that he is not only Carnatic Sangeeta *vidwan* but possesses fair scholarship in music of other systems also. On many points, his elucidation, though short, was an eye-opener even to those who dealt with some subject, by way of papers or demonstrations.

Dr. Padma Subramaniam is an outstanding dance exponent. She was slated to present a Bharatnatya Programme in the Music Academy, on an evening, during the 1978-1979 Conference, presided over by Dr. Balamuralikrshna. In the midst of her programme she announced that she would next do a novel number — Suka Lasyam — that is, dancing to *raga* alapana. This was really; a new and difficult venture, not attempted earlier by any dancer. The auditorium was full of *vidwans* and *rasikas*. Dr. Padma extended an invitation to the musicians "I am proud to see the galaxy of leading *vidwans* here. May I request anyone of you to come on to the stage and do *raga* Alapana and help me to perform the 'Suka Lasyam'. But none rose up from the seat. As time was passing, the dancer again spoke, "What a surprise? Is there nobody who could come over here?" Dr. Balamuralikrshna looked all around but none seemed to get up and so he went to the platform and started singing a *raga* Alapana and Dr. Padma did her part so exquisitely. When he switched over to execute *brigas* (fast *Tans*), the dancer managed to continue, though not with ease. The *brigas* were at such an incredible speed. A thunderous applause greeted both the performers. Other *vidwans* came to Balamuralikrshna and showered accolades on him, with the words, "You are the only *vidwan* capable of doing this, meeting the challenge boldly and successfully", However in their heart they spoke the words, "Without minding that he is the President of the year's conference, how dare he go on to the stage and sing for a dancer. Were we not capable of doing the same? Why were we silent? So that we should not desecrate our own tradition!"

On 1-1-1979, the title of 'Sangeeta Kalanidhi' was conferred upon Dr. Balamuralikrshna by Raja Sir M.A. Muthayya Chettiar, on behalf of the Music Academy.

Balamurali had mentioned in his article that appeared in the Conference Souvenir of the Academy, that he has created some new *ragas*. About a fortnight later, the veena maestro, S. Balachander, with a bellicose gesture, took objection to this statement. He wrote a damaging letter dated 2.2.1979 to the Academy and also published his letter in some newspapers. He contended on these lines: The covetous title of 'Sangeeta Kalanidhi' has wrongly been awarded to Balamuralikrshna, an 'impostor', who has alleged to have created some new *ragas*. Creating a *raga* is purely absurd for it is not at all possible to do so. *Swaras* are only seven and with their variants, they become twelve or sixteen, as the case may be, and the seventy two *melakarta* scheme comprises all the scales that could be permutated and combined. Therefore, Balamuralikrshna's boasting about the creation of new *ragas* was nothing but 'fraud' and 'humbug'. To teach a lesson to the culprit, the Music Academy should immediately take back the title.

Semmangudi Srinivasa Iyer, the doyen of Carnatic music, joined hands with Balachander in criticising Balamuralikrshna and his statements. He too sent a letter to 'The Indian Express' and went to the extent of getting an extraordinary meeting of the Experts Committee, during the off-season and get a resolution passed. Surprisingly, Balamuralikrshna though a member of the above committee, was not informed, so that he could not verbally explain himself. When M.G. Ramachandran was the Chief Minister of Tamilnadu, he announced a scheme to give Rupees five thousand annually to creators of new *ragas* and set up a committee to examine and recommend. Semmangudi Srinivasa Iyer was the Chairman and S. Balachander, a member, though they both resigned after a period of time.

Verbal exchanges through the columns of some magazines from the rival sides, helped filling up the coffers of these magazines. It was the talk of the day in the musical arena and became sensational as the 'Raga Controversy'. Balamuralikrshna wrote to the Music Academy and also published an article, "Creator's Note on Creation", in which he explained his stand.

An extract: "The word 'create' literally means 'bring into existence' and the noun 'creation' is defined as a production of human intelligence or power, especially of the imagination. It can never be said that a musician or composer 'invents' a *raga* but a new *raga* is 'discovered' by him. The finished product is the *raga*, while the scale is the raw material. The finished product is the outcome of the raw material. In the same way, the 'scale' is permutation — combination of *swaras* in ascending and descending order.... The composer unfolds and expands a scale into a *raga* through his composition. The bare notes in a scale vibrate, pulsate and come alive through varied *gamakas*, subtle *srutis*, range of *sancharas*, *visesha prayogas* (peculiar musical phrases) and through the movement of notes. Here it becomes a *raga* in the hands of composer. He is the creator of *raga*, who converts a 'scale' through his creation of a song into a '*raga*'..... Here I would like to draw the attention to the article of Sangeeta Kalanidhi late Sri T.L. Venkatarama Iyer, in the 'The Hindu' dated March 18th, 1970. He has written, "But the most notable contribution of Muthaiah Bhagavatar to Carnatic music lay in the number of new *ragas* which he had created"........ To one interviewer, Mysore Sri Vasudevachariar, the great composer himself had once said that "I composed a piece — *Devadideva* — in *Sunadavinodini*, but only Balamurali had created the *raga* by giving life to the *raga*".... Finally I wish to emphasise once again that 'creation of *ragas*' means that a scale has been converted into *raga* with an individuality by a composer.....

The insinuations, prefabrications and challenges whipped up by Veena Balachander, through the magazines and letters to the musical fraternity were nothing but the outcome of personal Vendetta against Balamuralikrshna. A stone is nothing but a stone, until the sculptor chisels it into a beautiful figure. He could not do it out of nothing, but he is really the creator of the sculpture. Similarly one is deemed to be the creator of a *raga*, when he gives configuration to the skeletal *swaras*.

In one of the post-conference meetings, Semmangudi Srinivasa Iyer spoke about Balamuralikrshna in a filthy language. The entire proceedings of the above said meeting, including the indecent remarks of Semmangudi Srinivasa Iyer, got recorded by someone secretly and the tape fell into the hands of Balamuralikrshna.

Nobody could expect that a person of Srinivasa Iyer's stature would have used such an indecent language. Balamuralikrshna found no other way but to file a defamation suit against Srinivasa Iyer to the tune of rupees two lakhs. He felt that Srinivasa Iyer's action had damaged his professional career. In the meantime, the Academy's executive committee and council of experts decided to meet and discuss the case. Letters and articles on the subject, came form many scholars, in support of Balamuralikrshna. An article (small booklet) entitled, "Wisdom is Wisdom only for the Wise", was one among them. This booklet, in detail, explained the meaning of the words 'creation', 'invention', 'discovery' and so on. The *ragas* already in existence but given new names by some musicians and said to have been created were also cited. For instance, the *raga* 'Maduvanti' got another name 'Ambika', by Prof. Waman Rao Padhye of Kolhapur; 'Rasiya' of Pandit Ravishankar, Darbar Kauns of Manhar Barve, Lagan Gandhar and Malavati of Kumar Gandharva etc. The usage of the word 'creation' by earlier scholars had been discussed. "Darbari Kanada, Miyan Ki Todi, Miyan Ki Sarang, Miyan Ki Malhar were his (Tansen's) creations", so wrote Chandrasekhar Pant, in an article "North Indian Dhrupad Composers of fame", that appeared in All India Drama and Music Festival Souvenir, Gwalior, December 1959. Such quotations profusely found place in this booklet. Likewise, the *ragas* of the Carnatic school with the names of musicians, said to have created them have also bee extensively enumerated. e.g:

Hamsadhvani	- Ramaswami Dikshitar
Kadankuthoohalam	- Patnam Subramania Iyer
Niroshta, Pasupatipriya	- Harikesanallur Muthayya Bhagavatar
Prabhavati, Leelavati	- Rajaganesa Dikshitar
Anandavalli, Karpoorabharani	- P.K. Rajagopala Iyer

The author also quoted few lines from various books. This is from "Music and Imagination" by Aaron Copland: "The reason for the compulsion to renewed creativity, it seems to me, is that each added work brings with it an element of self-discovery. I must create in order to know myself and since self-knowledge is a never ending search, each new work is only a part-answer". This booklet was dispatched to all members of the Music Academy and circulated among musicians. The committee of the Academy specially met to take stock but did not give any credence to the cat-calls of Balachander. Letters from many musicians and *rasikas*, congratulating Balamuralikrshna over his victory in the 'Dharma Yuddha', were accrescent.

The *raga* controversy thus came to an end, but not the case against Semmangudi Srinivasa Iyer. As usual, it dragged on for a considerable time. Srinivasa Iyer, in a state of impasse, felt, he could not escape out of the entanglement, for, he had already started to repent, as soon he came to know that the recorded version of his remarks in the meeting was now safe in the hands of the plaintiff. Some of his friends were appalled and derided him for his rash statements. They offered to mediate and settle the affair. When they approached Balamurali, he bluntly replied that it was not at all fair on the part of such an old and senior musician, to have spoken, in an irresponsible manner, that too in the presence of many and therefore it was only right for the doyen to apologise. Without knowing what to do, Semmangudi Srinivasa Iyer, finally, came to Balamuralikrshna's house, accompanied by two of his friends. Balamurali welcomed him reverentially. Iyer felt extremely sorry for what all happened and in an apologetical mode, requested that the case may be withdrawn. Balamuralikrshna, asked respectfully, "Why should you, a giant, take the trouble to come all the way and climb the stairs at such an age?" Srinivasa Iyer smilingly replied, "Otherwise, I have to go a longer way to the Saidapet court. Further, there is no doubt that you are an *avatara* of Lord Krshna and it is only fitting to 'meet the lion in its own den'". Balamurali readily consented to withdraw the case provided Srinivasa Iyer comes to the court and gives it in writing. Srinivasa Iyer had to go to the court and gave an apology written, before the presiding judge who heard the case. The suit was withdrawn.

Very soon Balamuralikrshna and Semmangudi Srinivasa Iyer became friendly. When asked about this, Balamuralikrshna said, "Srinivasa Iyer and I have cordial relations now. I have great respect and reverence for him, since he is the oldest and seniormost *vidwan* of the present day. This was my position in the past too. I tell you about two incidents. Once after his performance in a *sabha* at Madras, a review about it appeared next morning, with scathing attacks on him. The critic Subbudu wrote that Srinivasa Iyer should stop singing forthwith. Srinivasa Iyer, agitated over this, sent word to the Music Academy to cancel his programme, slated that evening, since he has decided not to sing anymore. The Academy authorities met me and requested me to persuade Srinivasa Iyer. During the morning deliberations (it was the music season), I announced that I will not also sing there, if Semmangudi doesn't withdraw his note. This message reached him and finally, with hesitation, he agreed to sing, since it was a request from me. Another incident was this. During another music season, Tamilnadu was in the grip of severe drought and the Music Academy had announced that it would match the receipts of the concert which had the biggest gate collection and donate the entire amount for drought relief. My concert netted the maximum and Academy was to announce the same, before making over the donation. But I informed the officials, that, in order to avoid any ill-feeling that might be caused by such an announcement, they should give the honour to the Semmangudi concert (which had the second best gate collection), though my collection was donated". That is the generosity of Balamuralikrshna. He dwarfed everyone by exhibiting his big heart.

Balamuralikrshna is commonly considered by many as a 'polemic figure'. It is partly true, by his musical style, compositions and behaviour, he always marches proudly on his own path, which itself may appear 'controversial' to others. He couldn't help this. He is ever silent about the next musician or his music, but when controversy keeps knocking at his door, he could not rest tight-lipped.

Diffusing the Melodic Beams

Music is the only art that can calm the agitations of the soul, as told by Mazzini. The born genius, Balamuralikrshna, has contributed to the world of music, a large number of worthy creations - new *ragas* and compositions - that possess the power to calm the agitations of souls, as long as humanity exists on this earth.

Comparatively to create a composition may be easier than to create a *raga*. A *raga* literally means that which enraptures its listener or lends colour to his mood. The term 'scale' derives from the Latin word 'scala', which means a 'ladder' and as such, an order of ascending notes of music. A set of seven notes, both in the ascent and the descent is called a scale, in general musical parlance and go with the name '*Melakarta*' or shortly, '*Mela*' (Carnatic system) or *That* (Hindustani system). A scheme of seventy two *melakartas* was enunciated by Venkatamakhi (17th century A.D.) and all the scales by permutation and combination come under the fold of these seventy two. *Janya ragas* are derivatives from these *melakartas*, They may be obtained by dropping one or more notes either in the *arohana* or *avarohana* or in both; sometimes retaining all the seven notes, but in a disorderly (*vakra*) manner. By taking a note, not pertaining to the particular *melakarta*, using it occasionally or regularly also a *janya raga* could be derived. But still, all these will once again be mere 'scales', until life is fused into them, employing various *gamakas* and so on. So in reality, a *raga* is determined not only by its *arohana-avarohana*, but also, essentially, by the manner in which it is rendered, having rich emotional content. Before Balamuralikrshna, many others have also coined new *ragas*. Sri Tyagaraja is said to have created the *ragas* like Kharaharapriya, Nadachintamani, Suposhini and so on. His disciple, Manambucchavadi Venkatasubbayya brought out a new *raga*, *kuthoohalam*, while his disciple, Patnam Subramania Iyer innovated Kadanakuthoohalam. Even in the recent past, Harikesanallur Muthayya Bhagavatar was credited with the creation of a number of *ragas* like Vijayasaraswati, Pasupatipriya, Sumanapriya, Saranga *malhar*, Mayapradeepam, Urmika, Niroshta, Guharanjani, Kokila *bhashini* etc. Instances of *ragas* devised by few others are worth mentioning here:

Syamali	...	Mysore C. Rangaiah
Skandamanorama	...	P.K. Rajagopala Iyer
Hamsaroopini	...	B.K. Padamanabha Rao

It may require a number of pages to go on enlisting such new *ragas*. The *ragas* created by Balamuralikrshna are not only melodically appealing, but possess some speciality. We shall now see them:

1. Sumukham: This is a *raga* having only four notes. Generally, there is convention in the Southern system of music that a *raga* should possess at least five notes, to sound aesthetically. But this is no hard and fast rule, particularly when *ragas* with only four notes or even less, are potent with the essential qualities to please the ears. Even in the Hindustani musical system, there are some four notes *ragas* like Bhavani and Malasree, which are quite pleasing. Long back, Kakinada C.S. Krshna Iyer, a disciple of Patnam Subramania Iyer, had composed a *raga* only with four notes — s g p n — and named it as Sankari. Few other *ragas* with four notes are: Tirumaraivadivan (of T.A. Sambandamurthi), Nigamagamini (of Mysore C. Rangaiah), Avikari, Sudhakarapriya and suchlike. Balamuralikrshna's

'Sumukham' has *shadja, Shatsruti Rshabha* (augmented *suddha rshabh* of the H.M.), Prati madhyama (*Teevra ma.*) and Kakali Nishada (*Suddha Ni.*), being the derivative of the sixty-ninth melakarta — Dhatuvardhani. To illustrate the *raga svaroopa*, he has composed the *kriti* 'Mahaneeya Namassulive' on Vinayaka, with a beautiful Chittaswara.

2. Mahati: This is also a four note *raga*, taken out of the twenty eighth *melakarta* — Harikambhoji — with *shadja, antara gandhara* (*Suddha Ga.*), panchama and kaisiki Nishada (*Komal Ni.*). Balamuralikrshna has composed an excellent *kriti* 'Mahaneey Madhura Moorte', to portray the nuances of this *raga*.

Ragas with only three notes have also been successfully attempted by Balamuralikrshna. Two of his such creations are:

3. Sarvasree: 'Umasutam' is a composition of his in this *raga*, born out of the first *melakarta*-kanakangi. It has *shadja, suddha madhyama* (*komal ma*) and *panchama*. This *raga* has the possibility to be derived from anyone of the first thirty six *melakartas*, because, besides *shadja* and *panchama*, the static *swaras*, the only other note is madhyama and all the thirty six *melakartas* of the first set possess only *suddha madhyama*. We may very easily say or write that such and such notes are there in this *raga*, but the extreme difficulty to sing it would be experienced only when tried. Apart from the *raga*, the composition stands as a testimony to the phenomenal genius and rendering skill of Balamuralikrshna.

4. Omkari: This is yet another *raga* of Balamuralikrshna with three notes. Some old treatises on music speak about *raga* with the same name, but having different *arohana* and *avarohana*. But the present 'Omkari' has the same three notes — s-m-p — though in this case *prati madhyama* (*Teevra ma*) takes place. The parent scale has been given as Salagam, the thirty seventh *melakarta* and similarly like 'Sarvasree', this *raga* could be derived form anyone of the second set of the thirty six *melas*.

Ragas having only three *swaras* have been proved to be successful with emotional content, but only by the diligent manner of handling them. One V.P. Sivaramaiah of Mysore had given a demonstration of such a tri-tonal *raga*, with the name, 'Svayambhu Swara Raga' in the annual conference of the Madras Music Academy on 31-12-1964. Besides *shadja* and *panchama*, this had antara gandhara (*suddha Ga*).

Apart from the seventy two *melakarta* scheme, some old manuscripts suggest the possibility of evolving two more schemes. The first scheme would contain 5184 *melakartas*, by way of having the *arohana* of one *mela* and *avarohana* of another *mela* and when thus multiplied (72×72) it comes to 5184. I shall write about the second scheme at the relevant place. Balamuralikrshna has innovated a *raga*, called 'Pratimadhyamavati'.

5. Pratimadhyamavati: This *raga* is derived with the help of the scheme no one, mentioned above, from the 4126th *mela* — called, Hema-Kharaharapriya. The name of the *mela* suggests that the *arohana* is that of *hemavati* and the *avarohana* of *kharaharpriya*. The only difference between *hemavati* and *kharaharpriya* is that the former has the usage of the *prati madhyama* and the latter has *suddha madhyama*. The *raga Pratimadhyamavati* contains *chatusruti rshabha* (*suddha Re.*) and *kaisiki nishada* (*komal Ni.*) besides *shadja*, *madhyama* and *panchama*. The *arohana* has the *prati madhyama* (*Teevra*) and the *avarohana suddha madhyama* (*Komal*).

6. Vallabhi: This *raga* created by Balamuralikrshna takes both *madhyamas* and both *nishadas*. The *arohana* is straight, while the *avarohana* is *vakra chatusruti rshabha* (*suddha*), *antara gandhara* (*suddha*), *suddha madhyama* (*komal*), *chatusruti dhaivata* (*suddha*) and *kakali nishada* (*suddha*) with *shadja* and *panchama* are in the *arohana*. The *avarohana* is — s n d n p m p g m r s — the first *nishada* is of *kakali* (*suddha*) variety and the second being *kaisiki* (*komal*). Similarly, the first *Madhyama* is *prati madhyama* (*teevra*) and the next one is of *suddha* (*komal*) variety. The parent scale is Dheera Sankarabharanam, the twenty-ninth in seventy two *mela* system.

7. It has earlier been mentioned about two new *melakarta* schemes. The second scheme proposes to omit *panchama* and having *prati madhyama* (*teevra*) in its place. This set of

melakartas has been named causally, 'Panchama Varaja Dvimadhyama Melas'. On a lunar eclipse day, Dr. Balamuralikrshna, in a creative mood was at random humming some *raga* and the *swaras* suggested something new to him. By adding the required tonal variations to the *swaras*, he got the beautiful shape of a *raga*. Paying no attention to the order or variety of notes, he spontaneously composed *a kriti - Mamava Ganalola*. Minutes later, he named the new-born *raga* as 'Rohini', since it was a lunar eclipse day and Rohini is said to be the beloved of the moon. In this *raga panchama* gets substituted by *prati madhyama*. The other *swaras* are: S r g m m d n s - S n d m m g r s.

8. In the same above manner, using both the *madhyamas*, successively, and employing all other *swaras* of the fifty-first *melakarta, kamavardhani*, a new *raga* was given birth to by Dr. Balamuralikrshna. He named it as 'Manorama', although there is another *raga* of the same name, but with different order and variety of *swaras*. Balamurali's 'Manorama' takes *suddha rshabha* (*komal*), *antara gandhara (suddha), suddha dhaivata (komal)* and *kakali nishada (suddha)*, besides *shadja*. It is possible, without doubt, that a new *raga* created by one composer, simultaneously may strike (or might have struck) in the brain of another composer, at least, in giving the name.

9. Lavangi: This is a four-note *raga*, born but of the first *mela, kanakangi*. The order is: S r m d a s - S d a m r s. His composition is 'Omkara Karini'.

10. Mohanagi: I have, earlier in this work, mentioned about the creation of this *raga* by Dr. Balamuralikrshna and the composition 'Talavari Nisi' (Light) and 'Nee Namamu Na Jeevamu' (classical). This belongs to the thirty-forth *mela, vagadhessvari* and the *arohana* is: *shatsruti rshabha* (augmented suddha Re), *antara gandhara* (suddha), *chatusruti dhaivata* (suddha) apart from *shadja* and *panchama*. The *avarohana* is s-d-p-g-p-d-p-g-r-s. Here the second Dhaivata is of *suddha* Variety *(Komal)*.

In this connection, an important and interesting event deserves mention. He once had been to Bangalore to attend a concert in the Gayana Samaja and arrived there, a day earlier to take part in a seminar, held on the morning of 5.11.1982. There he announced that he wanted to present a programme 'Raga Vikasa' in a unique manner. He invited someone from the audience (many were musicians) to propose a new *raga* scale, mentioning the *arohana* and *avarohana* with the name or number of the *mela*. The veena meaestro, V. Doreswami Iyengar gave a scale, arising out of the twentieth *mela*, Harikambhoji with the notes 'S r g m p m d s — s n d p m g r s'. Balamurali hummed it for a second and began to sing the *raga* with cogent *gamakas* and pertinent embellishments. The whole auditorium was non-plussed, when he sang the same *raga*, in extenso, the next day in his concert, following the *raga* elaboration with a newly composed song. When some inquisitive *rasikas* asked the name of the *raga*, Balamurali replied, "Since the scale came form Doreswami Iyengar I name the *raga* as 'Dore' and dedicate it to this Samaja".

The *raga* name 'Mohan Gandhi' is his recent creation, in honour of Mahatma Gandhi, during his 125th birth anniversary celebrations. They iyric 'Satya Sanatana' by Narayan Agarwal has been tuned and recorded by Balamurali. The creations of such new *ragas* and compositions by Dr. Balamuralikrshna is a never ending activity. Like Mozart, his mind is constantly creating melodies, without a break. He creates and composes, spontaneously. It was Beethoven, who once said, "ideas which are new and original arrive of their own accord and are not the product of conscious thought..... Usually, I am not myself aware that my ideas are new until my attention has been drawn to the fact by others". As and when inspiration possesses the composer, new ideas spring forth in the mind of the creative genius, which gives rise to various rare and novel melodies or compositions. A versatile mind and a capacity to stir emotions engender a great variety of forms and genres and lead to their unusual implementation. Art is created or perceived not as much intellectually but more emotionally.

Nobody can say what were the compositions in vogue among the musicians, before the times of the Carnatic

Musical Trinity. Such a question put to Balamuralikrshna by H.H. Vimalananda Bharati, has been narrated earlier in these pages. After the Trinity, many other *vaggeyakaras* also contributed some new *ragas* and compositions. The very term *vaggeyakara* would not have come into existence, if there were none, who composed new songs. At different periods of time, different *vaggeyakaras* appeared on the earth and left their creations of the benefit for the posterity.

Only one's inner urge compels to create something new. To create new *ragas* and compositions is nothing but a necessity of the times. Repeating the same old *ragas* or compositions brings only monotony and is not always healthy to the progress of music. "A narrow and limited repertoire in the concert hall results in narrow and limited musical experience". The cine music director, Vasant Desai wrote, "If some useful work has to be done in the field of classical music today, crcation of new *ragas* and new compositions in old or new *ragas* in greatly necessary" (Music Mirror — April, 1958). Dr. Balamuralikrshna has endeavoured to do a significant service to the growth of Carnatic music, not only by presenting the older compositions and *ragas* in a pleasing manner, but also by bringing into existence new *ragas* and compositions. His contributions, whether liked or not by some, will stand the test of time, and emerge as priceless gems and march towards eternity. It is not enough if one creates, but the success and purpose of the creation lies only in how he communicates them. The words of W.J. Henderson about Brahms (World of Music, Vol. I, Page 321) is equally fitting to Balamuralikrshna. "The power of his symphonies is to be sought in the nobility of their thematic subject, the unbroken continuity of their development, made possible by the perfection of his architecture and the indescribable mastery by which he creates and communicates melodies and moods".

Generally, musicians who concentrate more on the melodic side may not be deemed to be experts in the sphere of rhythm and vice versa. Carnatic musical system has innumerable *talas*, with complicated, *angas* (constituents), though only a handful of simpler *talas* are mostly used. It would really be a test to one's rhythmic skill, to manipulate various *gatis* (gaits), in any *tala*, and to introduce mathematical combinations in them. There were and are a multitude of experts in rendering *Pallavis* in complex *talas* or in a complicated manner. Their mathematical acumen and rhythmic precision would raise the eyebrows of the experts. Balamuralikrshna is known to every *rasika* as a man of melody. At the same time, his doing *swaraprastara* in his own and unique style is always worthy of praise. It never lacks in complicated *swara* exercises, though 'prima facie' it may appear very simple and as yet another melodic line. But for everyone to try even a single phrase, as executed by him, would only land them in trouble, like getting an electric shock. All mathematical complexities may be found interwoven in a very subtle manner, without detriment to melody. This is a case of fusion of melody and rhythm. That's why, his *swara* exercises are always 'Tantalisers', trapping the accompanists. This expertise is a boon to him by God and became manifest even in his younger days. *Mrudanga Vidwan,* the late, Radhakrshna Raju's memoirs about Balamuralikrshna in this regard, have already been referred in the early chapter of this work. Even today, Balamurali's *swara* rendering is in same style and by virtue of age and experience, it has attained multiple dimensions. Similarly like the *ragas* he created, a new *tala* scheme has also been innovated by him.

Once he happened to come across an age-old manuscript, dealing about *talas* of the Carnatic music system. In one of the lines, it has been mentioned that *gati bheda* (variety of gaits) is admissible in *Sasabda Kriya. Gatis*, in Carnatic music are five in number: *Chaturasra* (four *matras* - and commonly used), *Trayasra* or *tisra* (three), *misra* (seven), *khanda* (five) and *sankeerna* (nine). 'Kriya' is the mode of reckoning a *tala.* The *kriyas* generally in currency are beat, counting with fingers and waving the hand. Among these, only 'beats' produce sound and hence called *Sasabda Kriya*, while others do not produce any sound and called *Nissabda Kriya*. Taking a clue form the postulate found in the manuscript, Balamuralikrshna evolved a set of *talas*, named '*panchamukhi talas*'. In these *talas*, all the beats (*sasabda kriya*) may be in anyone of the five *gatis* and other *kriyas* in the common *chaturasra gati*. Generally, if a *tala* is said to be, for instance, in *tisra gati*, all the beats, counts and waves will be in that *gati*, whereas, in the *panchamukhi talas*, only the beats get the variation. The difficulty lies in reckoning the *tala*, carefully. In two alternate *gatis*. Balamuralikrshna gave an educative talk and demonstration of his *panchamukhi talas* on 31.7.1987, at Bangalore, under the auspices of the Percussive Arts Center. In the same year, he recorded a Ragam-Tanam-Pallavi in *navamukhi tala* — the beats in *sankeerna gati* and the rest in *chaturasra gati*. Tradition and innovation are the two polar faces that constitute the basic drama of todays. In the case of Balamuralikrshna, both walk together.

Nestor in the Triumph

Violin and *mrudangam* have been used as accompaniments in any Carnatic vocal concert, atleast for the past one hundred years. The very first use of the violin for Carnatic music took place in Tanjavur, in the mid-nineteenth century. Before that, only *veena*, *sarinda* and *balasaraswati* (the last two, bowed instruments) have been providing accompaniment, as gathered from the records of the Tanjavur palace. *Mrudangam* has been in use, down the ages, for many other performances. The very first Carnatic music concert meant for the public in the last quarter of the last century and the percussive instrument, till then, was being used in dances, in Katha Kalakshepams and still later for the vocal concerts. Because of the potential to cope up with vocal music, to a great extent, violin usurped the place of the earlier instruments and is preferred by many stalwarts, thus gaining a status as an essential accompaniment. For the same reason, some of the front-ranking violinists of the present times started to be in great demand developing egoistic pride. They thought it would be below their prestige to provide accompaniment to anyone and whenever impresarios approached them, they opted to do only 'solos'. This unhealthy trend is being criticised by many, in the past few decades.

During one of the informal chats, Balamuralikrshna

was questioned by a friend, "How is it that the violin has gained so much importance and become inevitable in music concerts?" "Nothing is inevitable in this world, other than God. It is only our own misconception that this or that instrument is inevitable. All through the years, the *vidwans* held violin in a high place and inculcated a wrong notion that this instrument is inevitable for supporting them on the stage and naturally, the artistes, who handle that instrument gained much importance. I do not, in any way, demean their talent. They are great, no doubt, as artist. A viola and violin player myself, I know, how difficult it is to master the instrument. It is equally so in the case of one or two *mrudangam* artists also. Whenever one is more knowledgeable, more talented and more sought-after, he should get rid of false arrogance and egoism. If it is observed that any accompanying artist is not as he would be, we should not bother about them. That's all", was the reply, smilingly given by Balamurali. The friend did not leave it there and continued, "In that case, the violinists would go on insisting for their 'solos', in the future. The vocalists would only be at bay for want of violin accompanists". Balamuralikrshna said, "No! Not all the violinists would get opportunities for solos. No matter how much the violin could reproduce the voice, it is a mute instrument, after all. It cannot give you the *sahitya.* Would you be able to identify, on hearing such mute instruments, whether the song rendered is 'Undedi Ramudu' or `Vandadum Solai', the popular Tamil song? Compositions in our Carnatic music are mostly Bhakti-oriented and the purpose of our music is to inculcate Bhakti also, in the minds of the listeners. That is why, the vocalist is always given the prime importance and a seat in the centre of the platform. Take for example, an young boy is arranged to give a vocal programme and a seniormost *mrudangam* virtuoso for providing accompaniment. By virtue of being the seniormost, the *mrudangam vidwan's* name will not be the first in the order, and the boy's in the end. On the other hand, the *mrudangist's* name will came in the last, however great he may be, and the boy's in the first, may he be a debutante. The reason being, a vocalist orally presents the *sahitya*. Further, I personally feel, violin is not essentially required in a vocal concert, provided the vocalist is of high calibre, though its support is always welcome". The conversation came to a stop but not the thought about it, in the mind of Balamuralikrshna. He started to brood. Why not we dispense with the violin or *mrudangam*, the so-called 'inevitables' at least in few concerts, so that it could be proved that vocal concerts are quite possible, that too, successfully, without those accompaniments? As a trial, he presented a vocal recital in Srikrshna Gana Sabha, Madras, with T.H. Vinayakaram (Vikku)'s 'ghatam' accompaniment, in 1975. Next year, he tried the second step of expermentation. Dropping the violin and substituting it with *veena* by Tanjavur G. Lakshamanan, Balamuralikrshna gave a number of concerts for about ten months. Only a violinist could not be seen on the platform, otherwise, nobody felt the absence of a violin accompaniment. Some cynics started to deride Balamuralikrshna. They charged that in the name of novelty, he was abusing the time-honoured tradition. Music critics (particularly few who now praise him highly) most vehemently wrote about him. The role of the critic in the arts is one of significant importance. They must always bear in mind that art is 'ipso facto', highly subjective and one individual's enjoyment of music, need not necessarily be the same as another. Pedantic criticism is of no value. In case the critic is ignorant about something he could be better eloquent in silence, rather than resorting to venom of verbosity.

On the other hand, the violin community didn't utter a word, for they were agape! 1977 saw many of Balamuralikrshna's vocal concerts with N. Ramani, providing support on the flute. This meet of two melody kings, offered a delicious feast to fortunate listeners. But it should be noted that in these two years, he also offered some concerts with violin and *mrudangam* support, whenever so required by the organisers. In any case, he never disliked any violin or *mrudangam* artiste, but only the arrogant attitude of some. As is usual with him, he wanted to do something more unusual and started to give few performances devoid of any accompaniment, except keeping a *tambura* for providing Sruti. Criticisms condemning such concerts appeared. Some critics fervidly asked, "With what propriety is he doing all these ? Who gave him the authority to discard the violin and the *mrudangam*, which have been in use, for centuries(!) and traditionally? Does he think that these lonesome vocal solos would appeal to any sensible listener?". Quite contrary to the comments of the critics, the above mentioned programmes of Balamuralikrshna, drew large audiences. Some congratulated him with the words, "We have been listening to your concerts for a long time. Many a time we have observed you had not done justice, by way of helping your accompanists. We were unable to kncw whether they support you or you support them. Today, free from all disturbances, we heard real music. Did Tyagaraja sing with any accompaniments? We now realise how soothing and serene his music would have been". As for Balamuralikrshna, he never bothered about all these. He is always nonchalant to criticisms of any kind. It is not that he did such novel experiments only with the accompanists of Carnatic music. He gave some concerts with Hariprasad Chaurasia on the flute and some more with Pandit Ram Narain on the *sarangi*. In one of his performances at Delhi, he was accompanied by Mahmood Dholpuri on the harmonium and on the *tabla* by a staff artiste of All India Radio. To accommodate them, he included some devotionals also in the repertoire. As far back as 1960, Balamurali had given concerts with Arunachalappa's harmonium, at Bangalore and Dodhallapur, near Bangalore. They are still cherished in the memories of the *rasikas* of those places. Who is to give an authority? When an artiste has every right to choose some particular artist for providing violin and *mrudangam* accompaniment, does he not have the propriety to include or exclude any instrument of accompaniment?

Many percussion maestros, who were already on the top, while Balamuralikrshna started his musical career, have gladly accompanied and blessed him. One was Palani Subramania Pillai, the un-paralled *mrudangam* maestro. On a number of occasions, he had shared the platform with Balamuralikrshna. In one such concert, held in the City Institute, Bangalore, the *swaraprastara* of Balamurali and Pillai repeating them with rhythmic nemonics were in a 'brain-boggling' *Sawal-Jawab* pattern, Tanjavur T.K. Murthi, Ramanathapuram Murugabhoopati, Umayalapuram Sivaraman, Tanjavur Upendran and a host of other leading *mrudanga vidwans* as also, Kumbakonam Rajamanickam Pallai, M.S. Gopalakrshnan, Lalgudi Jayaraman and other such eminent violinists have taken part in the concerts of Balamuralikrshna.

It is common among vocalists to take utmost care as to who would be accompanying them in the concerts, for they think that the success of the concert is in the hands of the accompanists. Balamurali's opinion is somewhat different. It is true that the concert would be colourful, if accompanied by able artistes. At the same time, it is more true, that the confidence that one could make the concert a great success without relying upon the help of the accompanists is absolutely necessary for any major artiste. Why should he worry about the accompanists? Sometimes, for various reasons, artists of lesser competence may also share the dais. It is the prime duty of the main artists. to do two things: One—He should not expose the weakness or inexpertise of the accompanist; Two—without heeding that there is somebody playing some instrument he should go on giving his own music. This policy of his became obvious on different occasions.

The performance at Paramakkudi (1962) was in progress. Balamuralikrshna, after about ninety minutes, started to sing his own composition, 'Bruhadeesvara Mahadeva' (Kanada), at the request of the listeners. This piece is in *tisra eka tala*. The *mrudanga vidwan*, a senior in the field, started to paraphrase in *adi tala*, without noticing the structure of the *kriti* or the reckoning of the *tala* by the vocalist. Balamurali, not upset and beaming a sweet smile, went on and the *kriti* came to a close. Except for the knowledgeable ones, the crowd never knew what happened. Even after the concert was over, Balamurali was silent about it. The *mrudanga vidwan* asked him, "I don't know how far I was helpful to you", to which, Balamuralikrshna replied "What is this? You are a senior artiste and certainly you were helpful".

On another occasion, one of the front ranking and eminent violinists was accompanying a vocal recital of Balamuralikrshna, at Cumbum (Madurai district of Tamilnadu). Balamurali did a short *alapana* of Yadukulakambhoji *raga* and straightaway moved over to the *kriti*. By this the violinist was deprived of chance to elaborate the same *raga*, on his part, though, such chances he got earlier, for some other *ragas*, delivered by Balamuralikrshna, in the same recital. The always 'too highly thinking' violinist took it as an insult and simply kept his bow and the violin on the platform and did not take them up, until the 'Mangalam' was sung. The courageously confident Balamuralikrshna continued doing one or two more *alapanas*, *kritis* and *swaraparastaras*, all alone, as if there was no violinist at all. While all of them were returning by car, the violinist anticipated that Balamurali would ask him about his behaviour on the stage but was only disappointed, for Balamurali was only chatting with him, in a friendly manner, as nothing had happened.

Music in its present sophisticated form has its basis in the folk tunes. Balamurali imbibed an interest in the study of folk and tribal music also, when he joined All India Radio, Vijayawada as the Music Superviser. He undertook some tours also as part of this study and collected the tunes direct from the tribals and the folk people. This helped him to analyse the similarity between the folk tunes and those of the present day songs. Many devotional songs of the earlier periods have gained entry into classical concerts today. Some older tunes are getting refurbished as classical, though, the original composer might not have sung in the same fashion, since no authentic record about the tunes are available.

Balamurali gave demonstrations on this subject, time and again. For instance, Bhadrachalam Ramadasa, a devotee of Lord Rama, has composed many songs, though he was only a *Tashildar* and not a musician. In all probability, he would have assimilated some prevailing tunes, for his songs. Old people in some remote villages around Bhadrachalam, still sing the songs of Ramadasa, in their older tunes, as rendered by their forbears. Balamurali recorded them for his analysis and demonstrations. During the Karnataka Gana Kala Parishad's Annual Seminar (1987), held in Bellary, he gave a memorable demonstration on the tunes of Ramadasa's compositions. He, assisted by a group, sung first the songs in the older tunes following it up with the same songs in the current fabric.

'Jugalbandis' are novel concerts that have gained wide popularity in the recent years. *Jugala* (the corrupt form of *yugala*) means 'duet' or a 'pair' and any two artistes taking part on a same stage is to be called a Jugalbandi. If we take the meaning literally, concerts by a vocal or violin, in duet, may also become a Jugalbandi. In Hindustani music, for instance, violin and *shahnai* (or *shahnai* and *sitar*) have in tandem, been giving duet programmes, which are titled as Jugalbandis. If on the other hand, a harmonium and violin or viola and violin give duet performances, they are not publicised as Jugalbandis. It is not clearly known how and why, only some such programmes are labelled as Jugalbandis. But the recent 'Jugalbandis' of a different kind two artists belonging to the two systems of Indian music, give performances, in tandem. Each one renders music of the respective style. It is often stated that such programmes are intended to bring artistes and listeners of both systems together and closer, which would promote national integration. This is a generous and fondly hopeful interpretation of the commercial aims of the impresarios. By arranging Jugalbandis, the organisers cast a wider net to catch more fish! This, also helps the participating artistes to demand an exorbitant renumeration. Mostly, Jugalbandis are featured only with instrumentalists from the time of their inception. Vocalists in Jugalbandi is a recent addition, though, there was an instance, when a short Jugalbandi — like programme took place.

In the nineteen twenties, S.G. Kittappa, the most famous singing star of the theatre stage had the opportunity to listen to Pyara Saheb, a Hindustani singer, in the house of Veena Dhanammal. Kittappa extended an invitation to Pyara Saheb to come and witness his drama performance. When Pyara Saheb got seated in the front, Kittappa began the same song as rendered by Saheb, on that evening. When Pyara Saheb applauded, Kittappa invited him to come on the stage and sing. Pyara obliged and Kittappa repeated it. When another song came form Pyara Saheb, Kittappa fitted the tune to a Tamil lyric and sung, to the appreciation of Pyara Saheb and the audience. This may also be treated as a Jugalbandi.

The idea of featuring vocalists of two musical systems, came for the first time to the mind of Kona Prabhakara Rao, who was the Governor of Maharashtra. Besides being a connoisseur of music, he had great interest to scout promising young talents in Carnatic music and to promote them. He discussed the prospects of such a programme with the 'novelty fond'. Balamuralikrshna, when they once met. It resulted in the first vocal Jugalbandi by Dr. Balamuralikrshna and Pandit Bhimsen Joshi, in the Shanmukhananda Hall, Bombay, one of the largest auditoriums in Asia, with a seating capacity of three thousand, in the year 1977. Both concert-wise and commercially, it was a grand success, Following the footsteps of Kona Prabhakara Rao, many other organisers came forward to arrange Jugalbandis of this kind. Balamuralikrshna has given such programmes with Pandit Jasraj and later with Kishori Amonkar. A worthmentioning point is that while different Hindustani vocalists appear in the Jugalbandis, the Carnatic side is represented only by Balamuralikrshna. It would not be an exaggaration to say, Balamuralikrshna has the honour of being the only Carnatic musician whom his North Indian counterparts respect very much. The reason is quite obvious. His music is more melody-oriented emanating from a sweet and pleasing voice and he is capable of singing what a Hindustani musician sings.

Pattabhiramayya, in his old age, was leading a very happy and peaceful life with his son, daughter-in-law, grand-children and great grand-children, His affectionate son had climbed the ladder of fame and reached the resplendent summit. There was nothing more that he needed. He, who once went around the streets of Vijayawada, carrying his son in a bucket-chair, attached to the bicycle, now became attached to his easy-chair. Sometimes, he was a silent witness to the activities of his dear son, which often became the material of criticism by his opponents. He knew that his son shunned grandeur and would do nothing covertly. The son always respected and revered him. However busy he might be, Balamurali never failed to enquire about his father's welfare. He never failed to show the presents, titles and awards he got, first of all to his father or apprise him about the proceedings of any function. Richly contented in mind that the mission of his life had succeeded, Pattabhiramayya attained eternal rest on 3.12.1983. The person who brought up his son, with tender care and affection; one who, observing his son's innate talent and extra-ordinary aptitude, put him under Parupalli Ramakrshnayya Pantulu; the noble soul who had sacrificed his own pleasures without getting re-married — this great tree had now fallen down. He could have simply said, 'No' to his son's stepping into music, keeping in mind, his own younger days and the difficulties he underwent in the course of his pursuit. Perhaps he might have wished, fame and name which had not come to him, should certainly embrace his son. A really great man had now gone. Balamurali, who already had got grand-children, now turned himself a child and wept bitterly for the second time, after the demise of his foster-mother, Subbamma.

There may not be even a single place, within the four corners of this country, where he had not given performances — vocal or viola — and this is not an exaggeration. For some years, in the sixties, he was turning down all invitations from *rasikas*, who live outside India. His service in All India Radio was also hindering him to accept them. In 1967, he visited Sri Lanka and cast a spell over the lovers of music. As a token of their appreciation, they conferred upon him the title of 'Gandharva Gana Vittagar'. A function was held at Madras on 11.1.1971, presided over by V.R. Neduchezhian, Minister of the Tamilnadu Cabinet, to felicitate Balamuralikrshna, for his commendable service to music. Accolades from various knowledgeable people and a purse with three thousand rupees was presented to him. In the same month, the President of India, decorated him with the prestigious award, 'Padmasri'. Musicians and *rasikas* of Hyderabad and Nellore arranged felicitation functions, in their respective places and profusely honoured the awardee. Those from Bhimavaram who attended these functions took the initiative to organise a similar felicitation, in a grand manner on 12-6-1971 in their own town and showered accolodes on 'the son-in-law of the soil'. It was presided over by Akkaraju Vasudeva Rao, the then Minister of Information, Government of Andhra Pradesh, where a three thousand rupee purse was presented to Balamuralikrshna.

The citizens of Vijayawada planned to celebrate in the fifties, a 'Ganda Penderam' function for Balamuralikrshna, the 'son of the soil'. 'Ganda Penderam' is a golden anklet presented to an artiste of extraordinary calibre, whose accomplishments are widely recognised by the seniormost person of the community in the presence of musicians and *rasikas*. On the day of the function, Balamuralikrishna was taken on an elephant, in the traditional mode, around the main streets with Nagaswaram music. The procession comprised many musicians, poets, scholars and the public. A host of front ranking musicians spoke, in turn, about Balamurali and his virtuosity. The seniormost (then) living Carnatic musician, Chembai Vaidyanatha Bhagavatar had come specially for the purpose. He expressed his extreme happiness to present the 'Ganda Panderam', by his own hands to the 'unsurpassable star in the sky of music'. Bhagavatar was always an outspoken person. He said, "It is not possible to attain such a high pedestal, without God's benign grace. Some of my colleagues tried to dissuade me form taking part in this function. 'After all, he is an Andhra man, and too young to be honoured by a veteran of your age, was their objection. We have earned name and riches only by singing Tyagaraja *kritis*. Was he not from Andhra, at least his ancestors? Take me. I hail from Kerala, but Tamilnadu welcomed, accepted and made me settle down here. I am of the strong opinion - the question of area discrimination could and should never rise on any account in the field of music. Its true, I am much older than him. But, could anyone refute that this young musician is young only in age but not in his profound mastery over music? So, I decided it would be only fitting to honour him and have come here all the way". Making Balamuralikshna to sit on a throne, Bhagavatar lifted his left foot, placing it on a small stool, kept in front of the throne, decorated it with the 'Ganda Penderam'. Chembai had such a noble heart to accept and compliment real merit, wherever it be. A person like him could be only one among crores.

In the year 1969, Balamuralikrshna received a letter from Lata Mangeshkar, the famous cine playback singer. It read as:

"LATA MANGESHKAR,
Prabhu Kunj, Peddar Road,
Bombay - 26

D/Nov. 14th 1969.

Dear Shri Balamuralikrshnaji, Namaskar. Two or three years ago, I chanced to listen to one of your records. I have never met you nor have I ever had the opportunity to hear you personally but when I heard your record, I experienced deep joy and felt extremely happy. I must admit that God has not only bestowed upon you a voice but has also gifted you with a rare knack and art to sing in different forms. This, I feel, is God's blessing.

When I heard you sing, I also felt, as if I had been

listening to good music after a long period. I pray that God may give you a long life and continued strength to sing.

If, at any time in the future, you are planning to visit Bombay, kindly let me have your intimation.

With best wishes and kind regards,

Sincerely Yours,

(Sd/-) Lata Mangeshkar.

Within two months of this letter, the Melody Queen sent another one inviting him to present a concert in the twenty eighth anniversary celebrations of her late father, Pt. Dinanath Mangeshker.

Balamurali was selected in 1977 to be sent to Italy, as the cultural ambassador. During his trip, he enlightened the West, by making it known that Indian music means not only Hindustani music, but also Carnatic. His first tour to United States of America took place in 1979. A regular concert tour was undertaken by him to Malaysia, Singapore and Srilanka in 1981. The number of his *rasikas* and fans, (including many westerners) is ever on the increase, and he visits various countries, every now and then. As a globe-trotter, he continues to render his chaste and sweet music all over the world.

Getting an honorary doctorate has nowadays become so easy, particularly in the case of musicians. There are some bogus Universities, who send the certificate conferring 'doctorate', by post, to those who pay a prescribed fee. On the other hand, genuine Universities after deep thinking and scrutiny decide to confer such doctorates to great personalities, who have done a meritorious service in any particular field.

The Senate of Andhra University, based at Visakhapatnam, unanimously chose Balamuralikrshna for this honour, in an extraordinary meeting. The Chancellor of that University, while belauding Balamuralikrshna, on the occasion (3.8.1976) of conferring the Doctorate, said: "It is not the awardee, but only the award that is being honoured in the present case". This was the first doctorate got by Balamuralikrshna. Later, the Jawaharlal Nehru Technological University, (4.10.1976), the Central University, Hyderabad and Sri Venkateswara University, Tirupati (14.2.1981) followed suit, in recognition of his untiring and purposeful cause to Carnatic music.

While the President's Gold Medal came to him as early as 1953, when he was only twenty three, the Central Sangeet Natak Akademi honoured Balamuralikrshna with its prestigious award, in 1975.

Kings and nobles, in olden times used to patronise musicians, poets and other scholars by appointing them in their courts, as *Asthana Vidwans*. By this, these scholars, by not having to worry about the needs of their households, would go on producing their musical or poetical works. M.G. Ramachandran, the Thespian with an ear for Carnatic music, after giving a noble thought proposed to extend patronage from the Government to few deserving musicians, when he became the Chief Minister of Tamilnadu. In 1985, he appointed Balamuralikrshna, also with some others, as the Tamilnadu State Artiste, with a grant of a monthly honorarium and many other privileges.

Andhra Pradesh followed suit and made Balamurali its state artiste. As usual, some envious critics raised their voice as to how a person could be the state artiste, simultaneously in two states? Very soon, they were silenced by both the Governments. 'Sur Singar Samsad', Bombay awarded the title 'Sur Vilas' to Balamurali in 1976.

Almost every state in India, has the regional academies for music, dance and drama, in the respective capital city, financed and controlled by the Government. In Andhra Pradesh, there were separate such bodies for music and dance. Balamuralikrshna was appointed as the Chairman of the Sangeeta Academy. But when N.T. Rama Rao became the Chief Minister of that state, he abolished all these academies, with the allegation that they were not functioning properly. If the reason was genuine, he could have taken necessary steps to clean the grime. The abolition of the academies, was followed by the removal of the state artistes. Pensions to some indigenous artistes were stopped, by the closure of the academies. Instead of coming forward to help the artistes, suffering in dire circumstances, the Government acted otherwise, which was particularly uncalled for, when the Chief Minister himself was an artiste. Balamuralikrshna felt this to be an insult to the entire community of musicians. He was hoping that Andhra would excel in the field of fine arts, by the unstinted support of the Government. When this hope shattered to pieces, in front of his eyes, Balamuralikrshna resigned his chairmanship. He also resolved not to perform anywhere in Andhra Pradesh, From 1988, onwards he gave no programmes in that state, inspite of requests from his *rasikas* and friends.

Chrompet Saswata Nidhi Ltd. is a banking organisation at Madras, serving the people. Balamuralikrshna was its first Chairman. Tyagaraja Vidwat Samajam is a registered body of musicians living in Madras. It has its own premises and annually celebrates the Tyagaraja festival, besides non-commercial monthly programmes. Balamurali is the President of this Samajam. He was the President of Madras Andhra Maha Sabha also. At present he holds the same position in the Telugu Academy. When Brahamananda Reddi was the Chief Minister of Andhra Pradesh, Balamuralikrshna was nominated in May 1994, as the Pro-Chancellor of the Telugu University and he is the first member of the musical community to get this high honour. But he resigned from this position (on moral grounds) within a year, when N.T. Rama Rao came to power, for the second time.

'Murali Ravali Art Centre' came into being in the year 1973, with the central objective to celebrate the birth-day of Dr. Balamuralikrshna every year on 6th July and also to honour eminent personalities, with the title 'Nada Sudharnava'. The number of awardees in about a decade's time, is seventy. Moreover, the centre brought out in 1979, a compendium of raga-scales (more than 3000) with the *arohana* and *avarohana*, collected from various music books and manuscripts with the name, 'Palai Azhi'. Some cassettes with Balamuralikrshna's vocal rendering have also been manufactured and released by centre.

Balamuralikrshna's mother was staunch follower of Gandhian principles and spent her leisure in weaving *khadi* on the *charka*. One of her regular prayers to God was that this country should soon become independent. It is natural that the son also imbibed the same patriotic feeling in his blood. When the country was provoked to wage a war against China; Balamuralikrshna volunteered to give benefit performances for the National Defence Fund, at many places, himself receiving no renumeration. In Bombay, he conducted a light music programme where he composed tunes for some Hindi Bhajans and sang, in duet, with Meena Kapoor. On another occasion, he presented a similar programme with Sudha Malhotra.

As a born composer, his lilting tunes make him the heart-throb of the public. It has already been mentioned that the devotionals and light songs he tuned, while in the service of All India Radio, allured every musical ear. When the Akashvani Annual Award was introduced for the best musical production, it became the practice of every Radio Station to send one or more entries to the headquarters and compete. Balamuralikrshna was invited as a guest composer, to produce some programme, by the Madras Station. As is his wont, he devised one in a novel manner, never before attempted. He chose a handful of artistes, capable of helping him to execute his idea. First of all the basic *sruti* (the part normally played by the *tambura*) was recorded with each artiste continuously humming (with closed mouth) each of the four *swaras*, which the strings of the *tambura* would produce. In the same method the sounds of *veena*, violin, *mrudangam* etc. were orally produced, in accompaniment to the songs. For this purpose, Balamurali selected the story, 'Andal Kalyanam'. The whole opera was an oral presentation, without the use of any instrument.

Though the process was time consuming and laborious, the opera, throughout, sounded as if all the instruments were actually being used. On listening to it later, some *rasikas* doubted whether it could be possible to produce such a programme since it was difficult to believe that no instruments were used at all. No wonder, Balamuralikrshna bagged the first prize.

Until about a decade ago, gramophone discs were greatly in use. Balamuralikrshna cut many discs, in which, he has rendered classicals, devotionals and also light songs. With the advent of cassettes, gramophone records started to fade out, slowly. Various cassette producers approached Balamurali for recording his music. He obliged HMV, AVM, Inreco, Echo and many other companies, though, most of his recordings are being brought out by the Master Recording Company, with the brand name 'Sangeeta'. It will be arduous to list all the songs, he has so far rendered on the cassettes. Suffice it to say that they include.

Tyagaraja Kritis (which also include the Pancharatnas, Utsava Sampradaya, Divyanama, Nauka Charitram, the opera and so on.)

Muthuswami Dikshitar Kritis (including the Navavarana and Navagraha Kritis)

Syama Sastri Kritis

Purandaradasa Devaranamas

Kanakadasa Devaranamas

Annmacharya Keertanas

Bhadrachalam Ramadasa Keertanas

Kshetragna Padas

Jayadeva Ashtapadis

Narayana Teertha's 'Krshna Leela Tarangini'

Compositions of Prayaga Rangadas (his maternal grandfather)

Contemporary classical compositions

Own Compositions

Tilianas (own)

Ragam-Tanam-Pallavi (in various *ragas* and *talas* including Navamukhi)

Tatvams (two volumes)

Sri Bhagavad Geeta

Adi Sankara's Strotavali

Songs on Sri Raghavendra

Songs on various deities (Vinayaka, Devi, Ayyappa and so on)

Songs for Bhartanatya

Suprabhatams on various gods (including the one on Sri Tyagaraja)

Besides, three of his cassettes have each been titled 'Sankarabharanam', 'Todi' and 'Kalyani'. He has exclusively handled one *raga*, for one cassette, respectively. 'Raganga Ravali' is an album of nine cassettes, containing his precious seventy two *mela raga kritis*. While once speaking about his recording these songs, he jocularly commented, "This would stop those - and there are such people - who might later say that I did not compose these songs or even that I did not know how to sing. In fact, I would like to make a video recording of these songs which will show that it was indeed Balamuralikrshna who composed and sang them!"

His songs rendered on the cassettes are in a number of languages - Tamil, Telugu, Kannada, Sanskrit, Malayalam and Hindi. 'Tanugu Talli' is the title of a cassette, in which he has rendered some patriotic songs, in Telugu. 'Ek Sur' — a video-cum audio cassette — often telecast or broadcast, portrays National Integration and Balamurali has sung in it, as also few others. "Music is the only sensual gratification in which mankind may indulge to excess without injury to their moral or religious feelings" -Joseph Addison.

As a *Guru*, Balamuralikrshna is exemplary. His method

of imparting music to his students differs from others, in many respects. Most of the time, he would be busy touring many places, for his programmes. While in his home-place, he never fails to devote time to his disciples, for classes. He would take up any song, he proposes to teach, only after explaining the *raga lakashana* (*lakshana* means not only the *arohana* and *avarohana*) theoretical names of the *gamakas* to be employed, in order to project the *swaroopa* of the *raga*, with a practical demonstration of them, then the meaning of the *Sahitya* and other salient features). If, for instance, a Tyagaraja *kriti* is taken up, Balamurali would cite some other *kritis* of the same composer, highlighting the starting *swara* in each one of them and so on. In the next session, the song will be taught, in extenso, with insistence upon producing the tonal variations. He is very emphatic that student should concentrate on cadence (soft or hard touch of the notes), while rendering the piece and would never compromise on that, whatsoever. After the song has been fully taught, Balamurali would narrate the circumstance under which the particular song came into existence and advise the student to always bear in mind, the mood of the song, whenever it is rendered. The third session, usually after the student is ready with the song, will be of quite interesting nature — a question and answer time. Doubts, if any, would then and there be cleared in this session.

The traditional Gurukula method of teaching and learning has become out-dated, though it had some advantages. A *guru* speaking with the student keeping silent all the time or the student obediently doing a duplication of what is taught does not serve the purpose. It may help only to learn songs but not any further. This method with its slant towards the dissemination of knowledge and one-sided monopolisation of activity has really reduced the students to a pitiable state of passive learners. The community of students were discouraged and ill-prepared to exercise their own analytical powers and communication skills. Balamurali used to say, "The time has come to shed this old attitude and instead to focus on how to make students think, analyse and question on their own. In fact in the olden days students developed a fear of the *guru* and they had no guts to ask, even when they were beset with doubts. Why a feeling of fear towards the *guru*? It should only be respect, reverence and obedience. There must be a friendly relationship between the teacher and the taught. The *guru* should behave as a catalyst in promoting question — nswer sessions, group discussions etc. Blind memorisation and rote learning might have been rewarded in earlier times, but not today." Balamuralikrshna's teaching process has another uniqueness. First of all he would make sure about the potential, voice culture and aptitude of the student. Then he would accordingly teach each of them. Some would be taught heavy classical songs, while some others, songs in lighter *ragas*. Whenever a new student comes to him, he would put the questions, as if in an interview, "Why do you want to learn music? What is your aim, to become a concert singer or to become a teacher? Why do you wish to learn from me and what is the special reason for that?" With the help of the answers he gets, he would decide the curriculum to be adopted. In this connection, I wish to cite my own case. I told him when I first went to him in 1957, that I wanted to learn maximum number of songs possible and also the art of composing music from him, but had not even an iota of desire to become a concertician. By further questioning, he understood that my mind was bent more upon taking up research in music. He then started the lessons - classical music, light music and musicology - and I was with him upto 5 April, 1963. He would tell me many a time, "A musicologist without knowing how to sing or play on instruments is not at all worthy of that name. Anybody can write or speak on various subjects in music, but to demonstrate oneself is necessary. I have taught you hundred and more classical compositions, as also, many light songs. You are fit to take up a regular musician's career but since you opt only for musicology, you may proceed on that path. Professional vocalists are increasing day by day, but not real musicologists. Delve into the ocean of musical manuscripts and other material and make a mark in that field". Only this beacon-light illuminates my path and would continue to do so forever.

Many learnt music from him as his regular disciples, while some others did it for a short period of time. D. Panduranga Raju, V.B. Kanakadurga, M. Chittaranjan, Jayan Vijayan Brothers, Prapancham Seetaram, P. Jayachandran (cine playback singer), Poornachander, G. Balakrshna Prasad, Mohana Krshna, B. Neeraja, K. Muralikrshna, Manda Balarama Sarma, Kurnool Chandramurali, Madurai Balasubramaniam and many more, besides myself. The cine star, Kamal Hasan, Vaiyajantimala Bali and the famous dancer, Kamala Lakshmanan have also learnt from him for some time. This list is not exhaustive.

Music is an art, one acquires, the object of the art (amongst others) being, the transformation of one's self from the philistine level to a cultured one. Every musician is destined to get certain performing opportunities. In the short span of a musician's life, he is apathetic to develop the art, but strives hard and spends much of his time, worrying about the number of performances the next musician gets and more about the remuneration of others. He stoops to the level of talking unfavourably about his own musical brethren. In most of the cases, the musician tries to shine more as a 'politician', than as a 'musician'. He takes pains to develop a group of 'fans', who would care only to attend his concerts. One may like a particular artiste's music and love to repeatedly attend that artiste's performances or listen to his or her cassettes - nothing wrong in it. But a listener, if he is an ideal listener, should never speak ill about another's music but perhaps does so, sinisterly by his 'musician' hero. This unhealthy trend of 'groupism' has attained a bizarre mushroom growth in the present times.

Music Sabhas are said to be the bridges that connect a musician and a *rasika*. These have developed up to a great extent, with enormous funds, large auditoriums and so on, but also as exploiters of the services of musicians. The belligerent attitude of some Sabha organisers towards the 'not so popular' musicians is pathetic.

Instead of an organiser going in search of a musician, it is the other way about and which has become the order of the day. All this happens only because the professional musician seeks to increase the number of his public appearances putting himself at the mercy of the Sabhas. Until a musician's performing is truly professional, such weeds could not be warded off. Of course, there are exceptions to all these though they are very few. Balamurali was not at all happy over these trends. For a long time, he had been giving a serious thought to these problems. A single individual cannot change the entire community, so easily. Realising this, he finally decided to 'professionally retire' in 1983. This 'professional' retirement, according to him, forbids him from performing in Sabhas mainly. He would sing in Governmental functions or at any place, sponsored by the Government. Further, he happily gives consent for benefit performances, if the amount raised is used to celebrate a poor girl's marriage or for any such charitable purpose. This retirement does not involve his singing in the wedding celebrations of his close associates, on cassettes, for films and in All India Radio and Doordarshan. Whatever amount he gets through these 'non-professional' engagements, goes to his 'Music Therapy Research Project.'

Our ancient treatises on music say that *swaras* have certain powers. *Swaras* are concrete manifestations of sound and the vibrations possess the power, that is how, *mantras* came into existence. They could control the elements. We are told that fire broke out, when Tansen sang the *raga* Deepak and torrential rain poured in a drought-hit area, when Muthuswami Dikshitar, one among the Carnatic Musical Trinity, sang the *raga*, Amrtavarshini. These two *ragas* are, even today, sung by many, but no such miracles happens. The reason may be simple. Every note has vital (or life) point and it needs to be identified, which is possible only by resorting to *nadopasana* (meditation on musical sound). In the case of a few, God endows the faculty to spot them out, within a short time. Since a vast majority of musicians use music as means for livelihood, they are deprived of doing *nadopasana*, and hence, it is not their fault, if rains do not pour or fire does not break out, when they sing these *ragas*. If the *swaras* have the power to control all elements in the Universe, they must certainly possess an efficacy to act over the organic properties also. Charles Darwin seems to have carried on certain experiments by playing the bassoon close to a sensitive plant. Pfaffer also has mentioned in his work, "The Physiology of Plants" (1905 - Vol. III, P. 79) about his attempts to stimulate the stamens of Cynareae by sound waves. In the ninteen fifties, Dr. T.C.N. Singh of the Botany Department, Annamalai University, conducted a number of experiments on plants, with the help of music. He found that Balsom Plants were excited when the *raga* Mayamalavagaual was played on the violin and many such other observations were made. Another finding was that the *raga*, Charukesi, helps to increase the growth of paddy. The effect of sound is similar in respect of human physiology also. Musical sound is said to possess therapeutic power. There was a manuscript in the Saraswati Mahal Library, Tanjavur, entitled 'Raga Chikitsa' (Treatement through *ragas*). The text deals with human diseases and treating them with the help of *raga* music.

Balamuralikrshna had experienced, even while he was young, that disorders like headache and stomach ache had vanished, in the case of some old people, after listening to music, for some time. He pondered over the possibilities of experimenting further, on these lines. If the secrets came to light, how helpful it would be to mankind! Although he wished it, he could not devote enough time to take it up, for, he was too busy 'professionally.' To do research on any subject, one has to study, concentrate and experiment, without the botheration of time constraints. After retiring from 'professional' music, he now planned to go ahead with his research. On an auspicious day, he embarked on the 'Music Therapy Research' project and has acquired many rare and valuable manuscripts, connected with 'Musical Therapeutics' and a deep study is now being undertaken.

Balamuralikrshna, endowed with a cultured and mellifluous voice was sought after by film producers and music directors to sing 'playback' in the movies. At the outset, he was reluctant, since he thought, singing in movies might affect his prime and chosen career as a classical musician. But he was continuously requested and finally accepted the offers. He has sung in many Telugu, Tamil, Kannada and Malayalm films, numbering about 126. In 1987, he got the 'Best Playback Singer' Award.

Many, well trained in Carnatic music, initially unable to set foot in that field, resorted to singing 'playbacks' and only after earning a name and wealth on the Silver Screen, slowly emerged on to the Carnatic music scene. Balamurali was but different. After a well established career in Carnatic music, he entered the film world, that too partially. Singing in films, with lesser strain, of course, fetched him lot of money. Because 'earning money' was not the sole aim of his life, he was not much inclined to sing in films, unless he got a compulsive request. His songs in 'Narttanasala' (Telugu) 'Kalaikkovil' and 'Tiruvilaiyadal' (Tamil), 'Hamsageete', 'Vamsa Vruksha' and 'Sandhya Raga' (Kannada) became extremely popular. The song 'Oru Nal Poduma' in the film 'Tiruvilaiyadal' is one, which is still a craze among the public.

In the course of time, producers started to request him to act in films also. Many stalwarts of Carnatic music, before him, have acted in movies. Papanasam Sivan, Musiri Subramania Iyer, Maharajapuram Viswanatha Iyer, T.N. Rajaratnam Pillai, Mysore T. Chowdaiah, G.N. Balasubramaniam, Veena S. Balachander and M.S. Subbulakshmi may be cited as few. Balamurali's histrionic talent is so highly competent that he has already acted in many Telugu dramas, broadcast by All India Radio and enjoys a proud placement as an 'A' graded artiste, in that category. To act in films was not helpful to him in many ways. He had to attend a number of call-sheets foregoing his concert commitments. After brooding over for some time, he decided to accept the offers, only if the role had a connection with classical music. AVM's 'Prahlada' portrayed Balamuralikrshna as the 'singing sage', 'Narada', who infused devotion towards Lord Hari, in the mind of the 'yet to be born' Prahlada. The other film in which he acted is the story of musician, captioned 'Sandine Kendina Sindooram' (Malayalam).

The third phase of Balamuralikrshna's film career is in music direction. 'Hamsageete' 1975 (the swan song of a musician) in Kannada, is one that permeates classical music in a sweet form. Another one is also a Kannada movie - 'Sandhya Raga' - (Raga of the twilight) 1974, which is infused with dulcet music by Balamurali. The famous film producer-cum-director, G.V. Iyer entrusted to Balamuralikrshna the responsibility of scoring music for his three creditable films — 'Sankaracharaya' (the first movie in Sanskrit), 'Ramanuja' (Tamil) and 'Madhvacharya' (Kannada). These were the three great philosophers, who estabilished the three religions, *Advaita, Visishtadvaita* and *Dvaita*, respectively. 'Sandhya Raga', 'Hamsa Geete' and 'Sankaracharya' secured Balamuralikrshna awards for best music direction. 'Talaivanakkour Talaivi' is the Tamil film, for which Balamuralikrshna composed the musical score.

The trend of the present day youth is evidently changing. They stay away from classical music, and grow up, unaware of their own cultural tradition and valuable heritage and succumb to film music or the superficial aspects of Western culture. A wrong opinion, among them is that the film tunes have no connection with classical music. It may be true to some extent, for, as in the case of classical music, no rigid rules pertaining to the use of *swaras* are adhered to in that type of music. The intention of the composers may be either to make the tunes catchy or to relieve the heaviness of classical music, in the films. Still, the youth are found to enjoy some old film songs and have a liking towards some popular tunes, which become their favourites, without any idea that the tunes have a classical base. Even for those, who are interested in listening to classical music, it may not be so easy to identify the basic melody of the tunes they love to hear often. Balamuralikrshna's interest towards the younger generation and insightful concern towards the posterity are ever obvious. He was giving a thought to educate and enlighten the youth and the neophytes, that whether it be light music or film tune, its roots lie only in classical music, in one way or other. He wanted to remove from their minds the wrong notion that classical music is 'sky-high' distant from them. Probably to give concrete shape his ideas, Murali Nallappa, a producer of TV serials, came on his way. Both of them discussed programme in two segments — one with classical music and the other with scenes from some film - was planned to be produced. The serial captioned 'Swara Raga Sudha' - a thirteen part module - was telecast by Doordarshan Kendra, Madras in 1986. It was ostensibly aimed at projecting the beauty of Carnatic music and making an impression on those who were still strangers to it. At the commencement of the programme, Balamuralikrshna would mention the name of the *raga*, that of the composer, whose song he was going to sing and the *arohana* and *avarohana* of that *raga*. He would then begin the song, after a brief *alapana*, Sometimes ending his part with a short spell of *swaraprastara*. Then clippings with song sequence from two films followed. This programme became very popular and 'Swara Raga Sudha', became an household word among the TV viewers. Nevertheless, the production had a snag. If the film clippings had been shown first, and the second segment was with the classical song, it would have done more to help the neophytes. The listener would have been taken from the familiar to the unfamiliar or less familiar. In fact, Balamurali's conception of the programme was only in that order, though it was probably reversed by the producers. But, the serial was effective to the extent that it led those ignorant of classical music to know that many film songs are (or were) based on classical *ragas*. The film actor, Y.G. Mahendra wrote to 'Indian Express' a letter expressing his appreciation. He wrote that "the programme created a new awareness amongst the youngsters. From experience, I now see children claiming proudly that 'Pattum Nane' (a film song-Author) is based on Gowrimanohari *raga* — something that they normally would not have been aware of, unless they went through the rigmarole of vigorous training". A multitude of such letters, bearing compliments, from various cities of Tamilnadu reached the Doordarshan Kendra. Later, the same programme in Telugu and Kannada were also made and telecast.

Titles and awards that Dr. Balamuralikrshna got are legion. About some of them it has already been mentioned. The Cultural Centre of Performing Arts, Madras (Sangeeta Sagaram—1989), the Indian Fine Arts Society, Madras (Sangeeta Kala Shikamani - 1991) and many other institutions have honoured him. He got the 'Haridasa Award' on 23.11.1992 instituted by Sri Purandara Foundation, Bangalore, in memory of the late, Vidushi, M.L. Vasanthakumari, in a grand function held in the Jaganmohan Palace, Mysore, for his propagating the compositions of the Haridasas of Karnataka. Swati Tirunal Sangeeta Sabha, Tiruvananthapuram, during its Golden Jubilee Celebrations in 1992, felicitated Balamurali with the title, 'Gayaka Ratnam'.

Hafiz Ali Khan Award, instituted by the society that came up in 1977, in memory of the great *sarod* artiste of the Senia Gharana, is presented to eminent music artistes of both streams, from 1985 and Balamuralikrshna was chosen in 1992 for this award.

The Government of India conferred on Balamuralikrshna in 1991, 'Padma Vibhushan'. He was installed as the *Asthana Vidwan* of Tirumalai - Tirupati Devasthanamas (which he later resigned, when N.T. Rama Rao came to power) and also of the Sri Sankara Mutt, Srungeri. Narada Gana Sabha, Madras, decorated Balamurali with the title, 'Nada Brahmam', fittingly, on 1.1.1995. This lengthy list goes on and it would be difficult to spell out all.

One day, in the end of May, 1995, Balamurali's phone bell rang up. N.T. Rama Rao, Chief Minister of Andhra Pradesh was in the other end. He requested 'Muraligaru' to forget what all happened in the recent past; to accept the invitation to come to Hyderabad on any convenient day and receive the honour to be done by the Chief Minister; and to revoke Balamurali's earlier decision and present a concert. The Chief Minister also said that since he had to concentrate all along on the political situation he could not turn his attention to the artiste's side. In continuation to the telephonic conversation, a letter also came from him, the tone of which was such that Balamurali could not say 'no' to it. He accepted the invitation and went on 5.6.1995 to Hyderabad and was honoured with a golden bracelet and silk shawl by the Chief Minister. Balamurali spoke: "By God's grace, I've been sumptuously honoured by the Government of India and various other institutions. I am fully contented. I had to resign the post of Sangeeta Academy's Chairman, not because, any injustice had been done to me, but, my concern was only the artistes whom I respect and wanted to help in many ways". The Chief Minister revealed to the public, saying, "Balamuraligaru is the pride of our Andhra Pradesh. Politicians may be praised today or abused tomorrow. But, Muraligaru is not a politician. He is the greatest cultural personality of our state. I have assured him that all his suggestions in the cultural side will positively be carried out. I also wish to make it known, he will, very soon, be reinstated as the Pro-chancellor of our Telugu University". After an interval of about seven years, Balamurali gave a wonderful performance, on the occasion.

A month earlier, Balamuralikrshna got another invitation from P.V. Narasimha Rao, Prime Minister of India, requesting him to join the Prime Minister on his trip to France, to attend the 125th birth anniversary celebrations of Mahatma Gandhi, organised by the UNESCO in Paris on 12.6.1995. Federico Mayor, Secretary General of UNESCO honoured Balamuralikrshna on that occasion.

Balamuralikrshna is a living legend. "Murali is Sarasvati - incarnate", in the words of no less a person than his own *guru*, Parupalli Ramakrshnayya Pantulu. His charisma transcends all geographical barriers and time.

Epilogue

An insuperable musician, possessing a silken voice, with a long, worthy and enviable career, a master of many musical instruments, a composer with a fountainhead of creative talent, always exploring the fathomless ocean of music, an exemplary *Guru*, an artiste with multi-faceted versatility, who has reached the acme of fame and aplomb by swimming against the current and a boon to the world of music, Dr. Balamuralikrshna is a prodigy blossomed into a genius. His innate musical mettle is a living saga and its reach is sweeping, through which, he has become one of the 'immortals' in the annals of Indian Music. This 'All time Great' might have 'retired' from the 'professional platform', but his musical contribution is perennial. The splendor of his soulful *swaras* will aglow forever.

"Murali! Balamurli!
Nee Ganaravali Sokina janavali
Annaru le Bhali Bhali!
Nee gundelo medalu Anubhootulennenno
Neegalamulo kadalu Navarasamulannee
Mai marachi Mari maree
Nee ganasudhagorli Mooga gontunakooda
Regunevo Ragamulu!!"

(Kavi Palagummi Viswanatham)

"Murali! Balamurli! The concord of your sweet music touched the inner core of the hearts of the people, in excellence. Well! Very well! Ecstacies stir up from you heart. All the nine *rasas* emerge out of your voice and make them forget their own selves, again and again. By the nectar of your music, even a dumb-voice would start to hum the *ragas*". (Free translation by the author).

CHART ONE

Genealogical chart of Balamurali Krshna

- Mangalampalli Janardhana
  - Venkataramayya
    - Pattabhiramayya
    - Janardhana
    - Appalanarasimham
    - Jagannatham
      - Venkataramayya (Wife: Seetamma)
        - Seetaramayya (B:1881)
        - Venkamma (B:1883)
        - Somanna (B:1885)
        - Jagannatham (B:1887)
        - Subbamma (B:1890)
        - Pattabhiramayya (B:1892) → M. Balamuralikrshna
        - Gopalam (B:1894)
        - Ramaanna (B:1896)
        - Lakshmudu, Narasimham (Twins) (B:1898)
        - Suranna (B:1900)
        - Radhakrshna, Lakshmikantam (B:1903) (Twins)
      - Mahalakshmi (wife of Bhagavatula Narasimham of Singaripalli)
      - Subbamma (wife of Kasibhotla Ramajogayya of Kadali)
      - Narasamma (wife of Veluri Sambhayya of Bheemavaram)
      - Venkataratna Sastri
  - Dasaratharamayya

CHART TWO

Sri Tyagaraja Disciples

- Manambucchavadi Venkatasubbayya
- Tanjavur Kannayya Bhagavatar
- Tanjavur Rama Rao
- Nangavaram Neelakantayyar
- Nemam Subramania Iyer
- Tillaisthanam Rama Iyengar
- Veenai Kuppayyar
- Neikarapatti Seshayyar
- Ayyampettai (Wallajapet) Venkataramana Bhagavatar
- Subbaraya Sastri
- Umayalpuram Sundara Bhagavatar and Krshna Bhagavatar
- Tiruvotriyur Iyagayyar
- Lalgudi Ramayyar
- Wallajapet Krshnaswami Bhagavatar
- Others

CHART THREE

Musical Lineage of Balamurali Krshna

Sivaramakrshnayya= Bhageerati

(sister of Tiruvaiyaru Rama Brahmam, father of Sri Tyagaraja)

Manambucchavadi Venkatasubbayya (1798-1827) | Subbarayalu | Krshnammal

wife: Mahalakshmama
(No issues)

Disciples:

1. Patnam Subramani Iyer (1845-1902) → Guruswami Bhagavatar, 'Poochi' Srinivasa Iyengar, Mysore Vasudevachar, Tiger Varadachari, Enadi Lakshminarayani, Salem Meenakshi

2. Vaiyacheri Ramaswami Iyer (1841-1898) → Simizhi Sundaram Iyer

3. 'Maha' Vaidyanatha Iyer (1844-1893) → 1. Triuviyaru Sabhesa Iyer —> Musiri Subramania Iyer
   → 2. (Umagalpuram Swaminatha Iyer → Maharajapuram Viswanatha Iyer

4. Tanjavur 'Lavani' Venkat Rao (1870-1990) → Tanjavur Sivaramakrshna Bhagavatar

5. Susaral Dakshinamurthi Sastri (1860-1917) → 1. Susarla Gangadhera Sastri
   2. Parupalli Ramakrshnayya Pantulu → Dr. M. Balamuralikrshna
   3. Mangalampalli Pattabhiramayya

6. Sarabha Sastri (Flute) (1872-1904) → Palladam Sanjeevi Rao

Glossary

Aradhana	: Religious rites performed to a saint
Arohana	: Ascent of musical notes
Avarohana	: Descent of musical notes
Dharma Yuddha	: War for Justice
Geeta	: A short song used as a vocalise
Kalpanaswara	: Swara rendition, done imaginatively
Khanda Gati	: One among the five gatis (gaits) used in Carnatic musical tala system. 'Khanda' denotes number five and as such, employing five matras for a single beat.
Mangalam	: An auspicious composition sung or played at the end of the concert
Nadopasana	: Meditating on sound; contemplation on music
Purohit	: A religious priest
Padas	: Words, used in a composition
Raga-Tana-Pallavi	: The piece de resistance in a Carnatic music concert. It comprises of three sections: Raga-elaboration of raga; Tana-doing the same in medium tempo, employing the syllables, Tom and Nam; pallavi a short lyrical line used to exhibit mathematical nuances, followed by kalpana swara rendering.

Sahadhyayi : Co-student

Sahitya Lakshana: Grammar for compositions

Samadhi pooja : Poojas performed in the burial place of a saint

Sambodhana : Addressing

Suka Lasyam : Extempore dancing to raga elaboration — a novel but difficult feat

Teluganya : A sect

Upanayanam : Investiture of sacred thread to a brahmin

Unchavrutti : Going around the streets or a place and seeking alms, usually done by saints and mendicants.

Varna : A musical composition with a lyric and swara passages, usually rendered at the commencement of a concert.

Vidwat : Proficiency

Vaggeyakara : One who composes both the lyric and music.

* * * *

Translation of some Telugu verses

1. Sri Vasundagu : "Prahlada ever worshipped and adored Lord Narayana was greatly tortured by his father, Hiranyakasipu. Did you not, when Prahlada cried, appear in the form of Narasimha (man-lion) and put an end to his worries?"

2. Vinalenika : "May be not this earth would see another (Harikatha) exponent, well versed in Puranas and music, such as this one. All good people of this Kali age are much grief-stricken by the loss of him".

3. Sreemantambagu : "In Tanjavur region, on the banks of Kaveri, (Ramabrahmam) lived as if a Sun among other planets in the Universe. His second son, Tyagaraja, even while young, mastered the essence of philosophy".

* * * *